Light
& Easy
Choices

KAY SPICER'S

Light & Easy Choices

Food for fitness, nutrition and fun!

GROSVENOR HOUSE

Grosvenor House Press Inc.

Toronto~Montréal

The publishers wish to express their gratitude to
A\C Alberto-Culver Canada Inc.
for their financial assistance in helping to make possible the
publication of this book.

Canadian Cataloguing in Publication Data
  Spicer, Kay.
    Light & Easy Choices : Food for fitness, nutrition and fun!

  Includes index.
  ISBN 0-919959-20-2

  1. Cookery.   2. Cookery for diabetics.   I. Title.

  TX715.S68 1985   641.5'63   C85-098120-4

Published by
Grosvenor House Press Inc.,
Toronto/Montréal
75 Sherbourne Street
Toronto, Ontario, Canada
M5A 2P9

Éditions Grosvenor Inc.
1456 rue Sherbrooke ouest
3e étage
Montréal, Québec, Canada
H3G 1K4

Printed and bound in Canada
Illustrations by Linda Hendry
Photography by Peter Croydon
Food styling by Kay Spicer
Cover design by Keith Abraham
Type selection by David Sutherland

Table of Contents

As a physician who has cared for children with diabetes mellitus for many years, I am well aware that one of the most difficult parts of their treatment program is the need to follow a careful diet. Eating the same amount and type of food at the same time every day can be difficult to do over many years. Breaks in diet routines occur commonly and are probably unavoidable with the type of lifestyle most children follow. Thus, anything which will make a diabetic diet more attractive and interesting should be welcomed by diabetics. Kay Spicer's new cookbook *Light & Easy Choices* offers a variety of recipes sure to excite the most discerning gourmet. She incorporates the latest information on food groups so that servings of each recipe can easily be incorporated into individual meal plans. I am sure that those who use this book will be delighted with the results.

Robert M. Ehrlich, M.D., F.R.C.P. (C)
Chief, Division of Endocrinology
The Hospital for Sick Children,
Toronto

Publisher's Acknowledgements

The publication of this book has been supported by Alberto-Culver Inc., the manufacturer of SugarTwin.

Grosvenor House Press acknowledges the advisory assistance of the Canadian Diabetes Association concerning the accuracy of the information on diabetes presented in *Light & Easy Choices.*

The publisher also wishes to acknowledge the Juvenile Diabetes Foundation for providing moral support, advice and encouragement throughout the development of this important project for the benefit of the diabetes community, and in particular for the younger person with diabetes.

Author's Acknowledgements

Writing this cookbook has been a joy for me. My thanks go out to everyone who has assisted and encouraged me throughout its creation.

To my daughter and fellow home economist, Susan Spicer, goes my appreciation for the hours and hours of testing, tasting and typing, and for enduring, with enthusiasm, the heavy work load.

I am grateful for the help and expertise of consulting dietitian, Cathy Patterson, R.P.Dt., who did all the recipe calculations; for the technical and professional guidance and counsel of Jan Eno, M.Sc., R.P.Dt., National Nutrition Consultant, Canadian Diabetes Association, Marjorie Hollands, R.P.Dt., Chairman, National Nutrition Committee, and Lynda Cole, R.P.Dt., past chairman, Youth Committee, both volunteers with the Canadian Diabetes Association, and Helaine Shiff, volunteer Field Service Director, Juvenile Diabetes Foundation; and for the assistance of Alberto-Culver.

I appreciate the opportunities Judy Brandow, Carol Ferguson and Marg Fraser have given me to share my creative cookery with the readers of *Canadian Living.* A few of the recipes in this book have been adapted from features printed in the magazine.

I admire the talent and skill of Peter Croydon whose "appetizing" photographs show off some of the food that can be prepared from my recipes.

And thanks to Bonnie Cowan for carefully and patiently editing the manuscript, especially the recipes; to the Lucinda Vardey Agency for their encouragement; and to my publisher, Grosvenor House Press, whose dedication to the idea of this book has made it a reality.

I also want to thank my family, Susan, Patti and Bob Jr., three well-seasoned critics, who tasted everything. Their frank and honest opinions about food and my cooking are always loved and acted upon.

Kay Spicer

Foreword

You don't have to have diabetes to enjoy this cookbook. It's for all those interested in their good health and in eating food that tastes great.

Light & Easy Choices was developed especially for the young person learning to cook and plan meals, perhaps for the first time. For the more experienced cook, the recipes are fantastically easy and convenient. Kay Spicer has shared many of her good ideas for cooking and preparing enjoyable meals that look as good as they taste. Family and friends can't help but want to join you in trying them. Best of all, Kay's recipes make you feel like a superb cook because they always work and the results are a big hit with everyone.

I wish that Kay Spicer's *Light & Easy Choices* had been available to me at age fourteen when I developed diabetes. It would have made diabetes a little easier to live with, for me and for my family too. Although my family usually ate the meals that were planned around my needs, it was at dessert time that I felt singled out. Everyone else in the family would have apple pie and I would have applesauce. Without anyone saying so, I felt my food was second class. If it was so good, why weren't they eating it too? With Kay's recipes in *Light & Easy Choices* I could have made a dessert the whole family would have enjoyed. That would have given me a lot of important comfort and support at a crucial time in my life.

When I read the meal planning section of this book, I instantly liked the idea of making menu cards for each meal. It reminded me of the way I visualized my diet at age fourteen. At home we had an old pigeon hole desk, the kind with slots to hold envelopes and such. I imagined that my meal plan was like that desk and that each meal or snack had a set of pigeon holes — three for protein, two for starch, and so on. Meal planning was simply making food choices to fill all the slots; an empty slot meant I must eat more and when the slots were filled in each food group, the meal was complete. The menu cards in this book show how you can put together many different recipes and food combinations using your own eating plan as a guide. The food lists of the Canadian Diabetes Association's Good Health Eating Guide allow you to have variety in your food choices while using the same eating plan each day. If you have diabetes, your eating plan is important because it is designed to give you the right kinds of food in the right amounts at the right times to meet your needs.

This book is designed for you. I hope you enjoy it.

Jan Eno, M.Sc., R.P.Dt.
National Nutrition Consultant
Canadian Diabetes Association

Introduction

The choices in this cookbook are light and easy. It is the way I have been cooking and eating ever since working on *Choice Cooking* for the Canadian Diabetes Association (CDA) and now for this new cookbook which was developed in consultation with the CDA and the Juvenile Diabetes Foundation. There is a lighter touch to all the dishes I create — less sugar, fat and salt. As well, I prepare them the easiest way possible. I like the nutritious, delicious results and so do my family and friends. They have become fans of my new style of cooking.

I am also constantly endorsing a balanced diet, like the one set out for the whole population in Canada's Food Guide, because I believe in it and practise it.

As I began to develop this collection of recipes, it came to me loud and clear that the Choice system of diet developed by the Canadian Diabetes Association is a perfectly good balanced diet for everyone. It is based on Canada's Food Guide and is recommended by both the CDA and the Juvenile Diabetes Foundation for young people and others with diabetes.

The more I read the experts and study research findings on nutrition, the more sure I am that the diet for individuals with diabetes is the healthiest and is definitely good for everyone. Mealtime is very special to someone with diabetes because eating must be planned according to the amount of insulin available to the body. Individuals with diabetes must have their nutrition in measured amounts at regular evenly spaced meal and snack times, in balance with physical activities. For a person with diabetes, food is a tool for controlling the disease.

Throughout the development of *Light & Easy Choices* I have purposely kept the use of fat and salt, as well as sugar, to the bare minimum. With all the reports of the effect of these foods on our general well-being, I'm convinced it is the most healthy way for all of us to cook and eat. Also, where applicable, I have used ingredients that contribute significant amounts of dietary fibre to the finished products.

Sweetness in the drinks, desserts and baked goods in my recipes is achieved by the use of SugarTwin, which contains the artificial sweetener, sodium cyclamate. I like its taste.

Artificial sweeteners are available in grocery stores, supermarkets and drug stores in the following forms:

❶ Liquid, available in a bottle, is concentrated; 1 mL (¼ tsp) equals the sweetness of 5 mL (1 tsp) sugar and has no calorie count.

❷ Bulk granulated white or brown, which looks, pours and measures like sugar, yields 4 kilojoules (1 Calorie) per 5 mL (1 tsp), equivalent to the sweetness of 5 mL (1 tsp) sugar.

❸ Packets, which are handy to carry for sweetening beverages, are also convenient. The contents of 1 paper packet sweetens as much as 10 mL (2 tsp) sugar and yields 8 kilojoules (2 Calories).

❹ Tablets which are in plastic bottles are usually sold 100 to a bottle. One tablet sweetens as much as 5 mL (1 tsp) sugar and yields less than 4 kilojoules (1 Calorie).

Saccharin-based artificial sweeteners develop a bitter taste when heated and Aspartame/Nutrasweet-based sweeteners like Equal have not been used in these recipes because their sweetening power breaks down in the high temperatures required for baking and cooking.

Choose the sweetener you like best and always read the label carefully to know how much to use for the sweetness desired.

A small amount of sugar is used in a few of the recipes in this book. People with diabetes are usually advised to avoid added sugar; however, some baked goods require the inclusion of a little sugar to work with the other ingredients — the flour, fat and eggs — to achieve the best results with the recipe.

When sugar is called for, it is there to enhance the quality of the finished dish and represents a small proportion of the ingredients. Its carbohydrate content and energy value have been included when the Choice value and kilojoule (Calorie) count of the recipe were calculated.

My recipes are simple and quick to make with easy-to-follow, step-by-step directions. All of them have been developed and kitchen-tested using both metric and imperial measures. The dishes are made from scratch with ordinary ingredients that are readily available in grocery stores and supermarkets across the country. A broad range of cooking techniques is used. I have also included some helpful hints, timely tips and slick tricks that should be useful for both the inexperienced and experienced cook.

The Canadian Diabetes Association Choice values are based on the energy (kilojoules/Calories), carbohydrate, protein and fat values given for a single serving after each recipe. This information is listed to make it easy for individuals with diabetes to include the food as part of their daily meal plan. The suggested serving size portion is the amount for the Choice value listed. People with diabetes are advised to measure and count servings carefully. Others who do not have diabetes can use the portions indicated if they wish to help keep tabs on their energy intake. Changing the size of serving will alter (increase or decrease) the food values listed for each recipe.

All the calculations for *Light & Easy Choices* have been worked out by Cathy Patterson, R.P.Dt., Consulting Dietitian.

The references she used for nutrient and energy values include the following:

Nutrient Value of Some Common Foods. Health Services and Promotion Branch and Health Protection Branch, Health and Welfare, Canada, 1979.

Nutritive Value of American Foods in Common Units. Agriculture Handbook No. 456. Agricultural Research Service, United States Department of Agriculture. Washington, D.C.: U.S. Government Printing Office, 1975.

Pennington, J.A.T. and H.N. Church, *Bowes & Church's Food Values of Portions Commonly Used.* Thirteenth Edition. Toronto: J.B. Lippincott Company, 1980.

Foods prepared from the recipes in this book are not only good for you, they are good-looking and good-tasting. Enjoy these light and easy choices.

Kay Spicer

April 1985

Kitchen Talk

Kitchen Math

Cooking is a science involving weights and measures, temperatures, formulas and methods.

While developing the recipes, I did the experimenting and testing. Now, all you have to do when you choose the dishes you want to make is measure the ingredients carefully, combine them as directed, and cook them at the temperatures indicated for good results, every time.

Measures for ingredients used in the recipes in this book are both metric and imperial. Choose *one* of the systems and follow through using the measures, weights and temperatures for that system. You may have problems if you mix the two, because slight variations sometimes occur in the adaptation of one system to the other.

Teaspoons, tablespoons, cups and quarts are the measures, and ounces and pounds are the weights for the imperial system. Temperatures are given in Fahrenheit readings.

In metric recipes, small measures, dry measures and liquid measures are in milliliters; weights are in grams and kilograms. Temperatures are in Celsius readings.

Ingredients are measured for both systems in exactly the same way. When the recipe calls for 15 mL (or 1 tbsp) of liquid or 250 mL (or 1 cup) of a dry ingredient, the measure is always level. I never use a heaping or a scant measure of any ingredient in any of the recipes.

"Always use a measure, never guess
Then cooking will be a pleasure, never a mess."

How to Measure Exactly

A good cook starts off with a correct set of measures. They are available in hardware and department stores and kitchenware shops. Graduated measures or cups for dry ingredients:

Imperial   ¼ cup; ⅓ cup; ½ cup; 1 cup
Metric   25 mL; 50 mL; 125 mL; 250 mL
Measures or cups with lips for liquids:
Imperial   1 cup; 2 cups; 4 cups
Metric   250 mL; 500 mL; 1 L

Small measure or spoons for both dry and liquid ingredients:
Imperial   ¼ tsp; ½ tsp; 1 tsp; 1 tbsp
Metric   1 mL; 2 mL; 5 mL; 15 mL; 25 mL

Abbreviations: g – gram   kg – kilogram   mL – milliliter
L – litre   lb – pound   oz – ounce   in – inch
tsp – teaspoon   tbsp – tablespoon

Measuring Dry and Liquid Ingredients:
To measure dry ingredients use graduated-type measures:
Lightly spoon flour, bulk granulated sweetener and granu-
lated sugar into desired cup or measure until it is heaping full,
then level it off with a straight-edged spatula or kitchen knife.
Never push it down or shake or tap the container.
Use small measures or spoons for salt, baking powder or
soda, cornstarch, herbs and spices. Stir to loosen in container.
Fill measure or spoon heaping full. Level off.
Lightly pack raisins, nuts, seeds and cut-up or chopped
foods, such as celery, onions, meats, and bread crumbs into
cup or measure until level with the top.

To measure liquid ingredients, use pitcher-style measures: Place
cup or measure on level surface, such as counter or table. Pour
in liquid to mark off amount required. Bend down and look at
mark at eye level to be sure it is correct.
Measure margarine, butter or shortening by packing it into
cup or measure with a spoon or spatula and then leveling it off
with a straight edge. Make sure all of it is scraped out for its use
in a recipe.
For liquids such as vinegar, vanilla, oil, juice and milk, slowly
pour from the bottle into the measure or spoon right to its rim,
taking care that the liquid does not spill over the edge. Do this
over a small bowl or saucer rather than directly over the food to
which the liquid is being added to avoid spilling in too much.

Cooking Language

These cooking terms are used in the recipe instructions. They
explain how to handle the ingredients.
Bake: Cook in dry heat in an oven or oven-type appliance.
Barbecue: Broil or roast food on a rack or spit over hot coals.
Baste: Moisten food as it cooks by brushing liquid, juice,
vegetable oil, sauce or pan drippings over food to add flavor and
prevent it from drying out.
Beat: Make a mixture smooth and lighter by stirring vigorously
in an over-and-over action with a spoon, fork, or whisk, or an
around-and-around action with a beater.
Blanch: Place food in boiling water for a short time and then
plunge into cold water to stop further cooking.

Blend: Mix or stir two or more ingredients together until mixture is smooth, or mix food in a blender.
Boil: Cook food in liquid over enough heat to make bubbles constantly rise to the surface and break.
Braise: Cook food in a small amount of liquid in a covered pan.
Broil: Cook under "broiler" unit in range or on a rack over hot coals or burner.
Chop: Cut into pieces with a knife or chopper.
Coat: Cover all sides of food with another ingredient such as egg, flour or crumbs.
Combine: Mix foods together.
Crisp: Make food firm and crunchy by letting vegetables stand in ice water or bread dry in an oven.
Cube: Cut into small squares, 1 to 2 cm (½ to ¾ inch).
Cut in: Work fat into flour mixture evenly with a pastry blender, a fork, or by cutting action of two knives.
Dice: Cut into very small squares, 5 mm (¼ inch).
Disjoint: Cut poultry apart at its joints, such as cutting drumstick from body of chicken.
Drain: Pour off liquid or place food in strainer to allow liquid to run off food.
Dredge: Coat food with flour.
Fold: Mix with spoon or rubber scraper with a down-and-across bottom of bowl and an up-and-over action until mixture is blended.
Fry: Cook in hot fat in skillet or fryer.
Garnish: Decorate cooked or prepared dishes with attractive pieces of food in a contrasting color, such as parsley, green onion, fresh lemon slices, whipped topping.
Grate: Rub food against rough part of grater to make very fine bits of food.
Grease: Spread baking sheets and pans with a thin coat of oil or margarine, butter or shortening to keep food from sticking. A small brush does it best.
Grind: Cut food, such as meat, into tiny particles by putting it through a grinder.
Julienne: Cut vegetables into thin, matchstick-size strips.
Knead: Work food, usually doughs, by hand by folding over toward you, then pushing away by pressing with heel of hand.
Marinate: Let food stand or soak in a flavored liquid to make it more tender and to flavor it.
Melt: Heat food to change it from a solid to a liquid.
Microwave: Cook food in a microwave oven.
Mix: Combine or stir ingredients together until evenly blended.
Poach: Cook gently in simmering water over enough heat so that the surface of the water jiggles slightly, but does not boil.
Purée: Process food in a blender or food processor until blended and smooth.
Reduce: Boil or simmer liquid, such as broth, to evaporate moisture and decrease the amount of liquid.
Roast: Cook, uncovered, by dry heat, as in an oven.

Roll: Move rolling pin over food, such as dough or crackers, to flatten or crush it.

Sauté: Cook in a small amount of fat over medium to high heat.

Season: Flavor food by sprinkling with flavorings such as vanilla, herbs such as oregano, and spices such as pepper.

Shred: Cut food into very fine slivers or thin strips with a knife or shredder.

Simmer: Cook slowly in water over enough heat so that water barely ripples on the surface.

Skewer: Fasten or close with metal or wooden pins.

Skim: Remove top layer of food from bottom layer such as fat from top of soup or stew.

Slice: Place food on a cutting board and cut across or down and away from you into thin pieces.

Steam: Cook in a container with holes over boiling water.

Stew: Simmer in liquid on top of range or in the oven.

Stir: Mix food with a spoon in a circular motion until ingredients are evenly distributed.

Stir-braise: Mix food as it cooks with a liquid in a hot saucepan or skillet.

Stir-cook: Mix food as it cooks.

Stir-fry: Mix food as it cooks with fat or oil in a hot skillet or wok.

Toast: Brown food by dry heat in toaster or oven.

Toss: Mix foods by lifting them lightly with two forks or spoons.

Unmold: Remove food such as a jelly that has set from mold.

Whip: Beat rapidly with a whisk or beater until mixture expands with air and is light.

Whisk: Whip food with a wire whisk made for this purpose.

Cooking Steps (Game Plan)

❶ Choose recipe and read it through.

❷ Shop for ingredients not already on hand in your refrigerator or cupboards.

❸ Set aside enough time to prepare recipe.

❹ Get ready, tie on apron and wash hands.

❺ Set out ingredients, measures, utensils and equipment.

❻ Prepare pans if necessary.

❼ Prepare food following step-by-step method in recipe selected.

❽ Put ingredients away and wash up. It is smart to do it as you go along.

❾ Enjoy at mealtime or snack time, on your own or with family and friends.

Safety First Tips
❶ Cut, slice or chop down and away from you on a cutting board. When using a vegetable peeler, work away from you, as well.
❷ Always wear oven mitts or use a thick, dry cloth to remove pans and dishes from a hot oven.
❸ Turn handles to back or side of burners so they don't stick out over the front of the range where they might be knocked and the pan upset.
❹ Remember to turn off stove or oven when finished cooking or baking.

Cooking Equipment

The following is the list of essentials I feel I must have in my kitchen for preparing the recipes in this book. If you have the same equipment, you will be able to cook up a storm whenever you choose.

For Preparation:
Hard wooden board or plastic slab for cutting and chopping.
Paring, utility, chopping and carving knives — and they must be sharp. It is also nice to have a bread knife with a serrated edge.
Vegetable peeler
Kitchen scissors
Grater
Strainer or sieve
Juicer
Can opener

For Measuring:
Measures and measuring cups for liquid ingredients, graduated set for dry ingredients, and small ones for both.
Rubber scraper
Gram scale for weighing ingredients and portions
Roast meat thermometer for checking the doneness of roasted meats and poultry

For Mixing:
Wooden spoon for stirring and mixing
Pastry blender for cutting margarine or butter into flour
Whisk. This looks like a group of wires in a balloon shape with their ends stuck into a handle. It is used for beating or blending.
Rotary egg beater and/or electric mixer
Table knives and forks for cutting and beating
Rubber spatula
Mixing Bowls. It is nice to have at least two large and two small

For cooking on top of the range or baking in the oven I prefer using nonstick skillets and baking sheets. As well, I find it important to use heavy-bottomed saucepans, especially for many of the dishes in this book which do not call for fat but instead use water or broth for braising.

For Cooking on Top of the Range:
Heavy skillets. I would not be without a small one for omelets and crêpes, about 15 cm (6 in) in diameter, and a large one 25 to 30 cm (10 to 12 in) in diameter.
Saucepans. These should also be heavy and it is great to have two or three, one of them at least 3 L (12 cups) for cooking pasta and making soup.
Steamer for cooking vegetables
Metal lifter or spatula

For Baking in the Oven:
Cake pans. Cakes, squares or bars made in 20 to 23 cm (8 to 9 in) pans are easy to cut into equal portions.
Jelly Roll pan. This one has sides about 2.5 cm (1 in) deep and can also be used as a baking sheet for cookies.
Baking sheets for cookies (preferably non-stick)
Pie pans or plates (23 cm/9 in)
Muffin pan for medium-size muffins
Brushes for lightly greasing pans and basting. I use small paint brushes with good hair bristles.
Rolling pin
Biscuit cutters
Molds or soufflé dish
Springform pan
Wide spatula for lifting cookies
Pot holders or oven mitts
Foil

For Storing:
Glass jars with lids
Plastic containers with lids
Plastic bags
Plastic wrap

Other Larger Equipment – *Nice to have but not necessary:*
Toaster	Blender
Electric skillet	Food Processor
Toaster Oven	Microwave Oven

Cooking Ingredients

The choice of foods in our supermarkets today is mind-boggling. Even a shopping trip to the corner grocer can buy almost anything we need to cook and eat. I kept a supply of staples and non-perishable ingredients on hand while developing the recipes for this collection. Then all I had to buy every couple of days were the fresh meats, poultry, fish, vegetables and fruits I needed. You might like to do the same. Here is the list of ingredients to keep on hand to make the recipes from this book:

In the Kitchen Cupboard
Baking Needs:
All-purpose flour
Whole wheat flour
Quick-cooking rolled oats
Cornmeal
Bulk granulated (white and brown) and liquid artificial sweetener, like SugarTwin
Granulated sugar
Corn syrup
Molasses
Baking powder
Baking soda
Dry unsweetened cocoa
Vanilla
Almond extract
Semi-sweet chocolate chips

Canned and Bottled Goods
Tomatoes
Kidney Beans
Romano Beans
Lentils
Chick peas
Soy sauce
Worcestershire sauce
Hot pepper sauce
Peanut butter
Unsweetened pineapple
Unsweetened apple, pineapple and grape juice
Catsup
Chili sauce

Dried Goods
Pasta (macaroni, spaghetti, lasagna noodles)
White long grain rice and short grain rice
Brown rice
Raisins
Dried apricots
Instant bouillon mix or cubes for chicken and beef broth
Seeds and nuts — sesame and sunflower seeds, walnuts, almonds, pecans
Corn oil
Vinegar
Herbs and Spices:
This list seems long. Buy one or two at a time. These are the ingredients that help flavor cooked foods: Chili powder, cayenne pepper, curry powder, dried basil, bay leaves, celery seed, thyme, oregano, marjoram, tarragon, paprika, cinnamon, cloves, ground ginger, nutmeg, cardamom, coriander, allspice, cream of tartar.

In the Refrigerator
Cheddar, mozzarella and Parmesan cheese
Dijon mustard
Lemons
Oranges
Green onions
Parsley
Unsalted butter
2% cottage cheese
2% yogurt
2% skim milk
Carrots
Celery
Eggs

In a Vegetable Bin
Cooking onions
Garlic
Potatoes

Meal Planning:
Make it a Game Everyone Wins!

When a person has diabetes it is important to balance the protein, carbohydrate and fat in a meal to control how much sugar will enter the bloodstream after the meal. The Food Group System with its Choices, used with a meal plan, makes this balance possible.

A suitable meal plan can be worked out with a dietitian who understands how to plan meals to meet your energy needs, taking into consideration your insulin and exercise pattern. The dietitian will help you decide how many Choices from each food group you wish to have at each meal. Then your dietitian's guide is your meal plan ... and how you play the game is up to you. The choice is yours and this cookbook will help you add variety to your meals. The Food Choice value for a serving of a certain size has been worked out for you for each recipe so that you can fit your favorites into your own meal plan.

The following sample menus were planned using different meal plans for Sammy and Ted, Jane, Pat and Bob — all different young people — different ages, different food preferences, different energy needs. Their plan for a particular meal may or may not be the same as yours.

Take your own meal plan (or diet) and write up menu cards in the same way, only using the number of Food Choices from each food group on your own Good Health Eating Guide. Decide what and how much you are going to eat at a meal, and then you will have a meal that is nutritious, delicious — and balanced with *your* insulin supply and *your* energy needs.

Recipes in *Light & Easy Choices* are indicated by an asterisk (*).

For example, your game plan for breakfast might consist of:

1 ∅ Protein Choice
2 ☐ Starchy Choices
2 ◆ Milk Choices (2%)
1 ∅ Fruits & Vegetables Choice
2 ▲ Fats & Oils Choices

Sample Breakfast	Food Choice Groups							Energy	
For: Sammy **Meal:** Breakfast 8:00 am	Protein	Starchy	Milk	Fruits & Vegetables	Extra Vegetables ++	Fats & Oils	Extra ++	kilojoules	Calories
Orange Juice (125 mL/½ cup)				1				245	58
Poached Egg on	1							330	79
1 slice whole wheat toast with margarine (5 mL/1 tsp)		1				1		300 150	72 36
1 Orange Cornmeal Muffin* with margarine (5 mL/1 tsp)		1				1		290 150	69 36
Milk (250 mL/1 cup 2%)			2(2%)					540	129
Total Choices on Meal Plan	1	2	2(2%)	1		2			
Total Energy Value								2005	479

Meal planning is as simple as that!

To plan a meal, first list the total number of the Choices allowed from each Food Group for that meal on your own personal meal plan. Go through the recipes and as you select one, see what Choices will be used up in a serving. Subtract that from the to-tal; then you can see what you have as you go along and what Choices need to be added to the meal. Be sure to count only the measured amount for a serving. If you want to eat 1½ or 2 serv-ings of a certain dish, remember to count 1½ or 2 times the number of Choices in your meal. Everything you plan to eat at a meal must be included in your game plan unless they are ++Extras.

This mixing and matching makes meal planning a game. It is a good idea to keep a copy of your menus on cards or in a book to help you remember combinations that you like and that work for you. It will be a handy and time-saving record to have at your fingertips.

When you use the recipes in this book with your own eating plan, you will be able to enjoy light, lively and luscious meals planned just for you.

Special Family Dinner	Protein	Starchy	Milk	Fruits & Vegetables	Extra Vegetables ++	Fats & Oils	Extra ++	kilojoules	Calories
For: Bob Meal: Evening 7:00 pm	⊘	▢	◆	▱	++	△	++		
*Potted Cheese in	1							230	55
Celery Sticks					++				
*Roast Chicken	3							690	165
*Grandma's Bread Stuffing (2 servings)		2				1		780	118
*Schnippled Green Beans					++			80	20
*Ginger Orange Carrots				1				240	57
*Cheesy Chive Potatoes		1						270	64
*Chocolate Mousse			1(skim)			1		300	72
Milk (125 mL/½ cup 2%)			1(2%)					270	65
Total Choices on Meal Plan	**4**	**3**	**2(2%)**	**1**	**++**	**2**			
Total Energy Value								**2860**	**616**

Snack Supper	Protein	Starchy	Milk	Fruits & Vegetables	Extra Vegetables ++	Fats & Oils	Extra ++	kilojoules	Calories
For: Pat Meal: Evening 5:30 pm	⊘	▢	◆	▱	++	△	++		
*Bunch of Crunch with					++				
*Basil Cheese Dip	1							190	45
*Mini Pizza (2 Servings)	2	2				2		1480	350
*Apricot Sherbet (2 servings)				2				200	48
Milk (250 mL/1 cup 2%)			2(2%)					540	129
Total Choices on Meal Plan	**3**	**2**	**2(2%)**	**2**	**++**	**2**			
Total Energy Value								**2410**	**572**

School Lunch	Food Choice Groups							Energy	
For: Ted **Meal:** Noon-time 12:00 pm	Protein ∅	Starchy ☐	Milk ◆	Fruits & Vegetables ◢	Extra Vegetables ++	Fats & Oils ▲	Extra ++	kilojoules	Calories
*Tuna Turnover (2)	2	2						920	220
Celery Sticks					++				
*Butterscotch Peanut Cookies (4)		1				2		760	180
Milk (250 mL/1 cup 2%)			2(2%)					540	129
Total Choices on Meal Plan	2	3	2(2%)		++	2			
Total Energy Value								2220	529

Week-day Breakfast	Food Choice Groups							Energy	
For: Jane **Meal:** Breakfast 8:00 am	Protein ∅	Starchy ☐	Milk ◆	Fruits & Vegetables ◢	Extra Vegetables ++	Fats & Oils ▲	Extra ++	kilojoules	Calories
Half Grapefruit				1				190	45
Scrambled Egg	1							330	79
*English Muffin		2						640	153
Margarine (5 mL/1 tsp)						1		150	36
Lo-Cal Spread							++	21	5
*Frothy Rich Hot Chocolate			2(skim)					350	84
Total Choices on Meal Plan	1	2	2(skim)	1		1	++		
Total Energy Value								1681	402

The Canadian Diabetes Association's Food Group System

Tasty, wholesome food provides great enjoyment. It also supplies energy and the essential nutrients for building and maintaining a healthy body. While people with diabetes have the same nutritional needs as anyone else, they must also balance the kind and amount of food they eat with their limited insulin supply. A qualified dietitian or nutritionist can help them achieve this balance by designing an individually tailored *Eating Plan.* Factors such as activity level, weight, age, medication and food preferences are considered by the dietitian as she prepares the plan and discusses it with the person with diabetes. An *Eating Plan* based on either the Food Group System or Exchange System can include meals prepared using this specially developed collection of recipes.

A comparison of the two systems is summarized below.

Food Group System	**Exchange System**
1 Protein Foods Choice*	1 Meat Exchange
1 Starchy Foods Choice	1 Bread Exchange
1 Milk Choice	1 Milk Exchange
1 Fruits & Vegetables Choice	1 Fruit Exchange
1 Fruits & Vegetables Choice	1 Vegetable Exchange, Group A
1 Fats & Oils Choice	1 Fat Exchange
Extra Vegetables	Vegetable Exchange, Group B
Extras (unmeasured)	Calorie-Free Foods, List A
Extras (small measures)	Calorie Poor Foods, List B

The *Food Group System* is a revised form of the Exchange System of meal planning. It is based on *Canada's Food Guide,* with modifications to make it suitable for people with diabetes. In the *Food Group System,* foods are classified into six groups according to their carbohydrate, protein and fat content. These groups are identified by different symbols.

*Dietary calculations are based on protein foods low in fat. If protein foods high in fat are chosen frequently, the dietary calculations would be adjusted to account for the extra "hidden" fat.

The word *CHOICE* refers to a measured (or weighed) amount of food which can be replaced by another in that Food Choice Group. This system can be used to plan menus for the whole family, but the serving sizes will vary according to individual needs.

These recipes have been developed in both metric and imperial measures. Choose the system of measures that you prefer and use the tools designed for that system. Slight variations sometimes occur between the two systems, therefore it is most important to follow through the recipe using one system — metric or imperial — only.

Nutrient Values have been calculated for single servings of each recipe using current Food Composition tables. These figures should be regarded as approximate due to the variations between tables and the many factors which can alter the yield of a recipe.

The Food Groups

Protein Foods Ø

This group includes meat, fish, poultry, cheese and eggs. These are excellent sources of protein, which is essential for life. It is used for building, maintaining and repairing body tissues and also forms an important part of hormones and antibodies.

When shopping for meat, select cuts which look lean and have little visible fat distributed (marbled) throughout. Buy enough meat to allow for shrinkage during cooking — 100 g (4 oz) raw, boneless meat will yield about 75 g (3 oz) cooked. When selecting chops or poultry, purchase double the weight required — 500 g (1 lb) raw poultry or chops will yield about 250 g (½ lb) cooked.

Protein foods low in fat are listed first in the following chart. Choose them often, especially if you need to lose weight.

One Choice from the Protein Foods Group Ø contains approximately 7 g protein and 3 g fat and yields an energy value of about 230 kilojoules (55 Calories). All weights and measures are for cooked meats, fish and poultry unless otherwise stated.

	Cheese	
25 g	All types, made from partly skim milk, e.g. Mozzarella, part-skim	1 piece, 5 cm x 2 cm x 2 cm (2" x ¾" x¾")
55 g	Cottage Cheese, all types	50 mL (¼ cup)

Fish

30 g	Canned, drained, e.g. Chicken Haddie, Mackerel, Salmon, Tuna	50 mL ($\frac{1}{4}$ cup)
50 g	Cod Tongues/Cheeks	75 mL ($\frac{1}{3}$ cup)
30 g	Fillet or Steak, e.g. Boston blue, Cod, Flounder, Haddock, Halibut, Perch, Pickerel, Pike, Salmon, Shad, Sole, Trout, Whitefish	1 piece, 6 cm x 2 cm x 2 cm ($2\frac{1}{2}$" x $\frac{3}{4}$" x $\frac{3}{4}$")
30 g	Herring	$\frac{1}{3}$ fish
30 g	Sardines	2 medium or 3 small
30 g	Smelts	2 medium

Shellfish

30 g	Clams, Mussels, Oysters, Scallops, Snails	3 medium
30 g	Crab, Lobster, flaked	50 mL ($\frac{1}{4}$ cup)
30 g	Shrimp – fresh	5 large
30 g	– frozen	10 medium
30 g	– canned	18 small

Meat and Poultry
e.g. Beef, Chicken, Ham, Lamb, Pork, Turkey, Veal, Wild Game:

25 g	Back Bacon	3 slices, thin
35 g	Chop	$\frac{1}{2}$ chop, with bone
25 g	Minced or ground, lean	30 mL (2 tbsp)
25 g	Sliced, lean	1 slice, 10 cm x 5 cm x 5 mm (4" x 2" x $\frac{1}{4}$")
25 g	Steak, lean	1 piece, 4 cm x 3 cm x 2 cm ($1\frac{1}{2}$" x $1\frac{1}{4}$" x $\frac{3}{4}$")

Organ Meats

25 g	Heart, Liver	1 slice, 5 cm x 5 cm x 1 cm (2" x 2" x $\frac{1}{2}$")
25 g	Kidney, Sweet Breads, chopped	50 mL ($\frac{1}{4}$ cup)

Soybean

70 g	Bean Curd or Tofu, 1 block = 6 cm x 6 cm x 4 cm (2½" x 2½" x 1½")	½ block

**The following choices contain extra fat,
so use them less often.**

Cheese

25 g	Cheese, all types, made from whole milk, e.g. Brick, Brie, Camembert, Cheddar, Edam, Tilsit	1 piece, 5 cm x 2 cm x 2 cm (2" x ¾" x¾")
25 g	Cheese, coarsely grated, e.g. Cheddar	75 mL (⅓ cup)
15 g	Cheese, dry, finely grated, e.g. Parmesan	45 mL (3 tbsp)
55 g	Cheese, Ricotta	50 mL (¼ cup)

Egg

50 g	Egg, in shell, raw or cooked	1 medium
55 g	Egg, scrambled	50 mL (¼ cup)

Meat

40 g	Bologna, Summer Sausage or Salami	1 slice, 5 mm, 10 cm diameter (¼", 4" diameter)
40 g	Canned Luncheon Meat	1 slice, 85 mm x 45 mm x 10 mm (3½" x 1¾" x ½")
25 g	Ground Beef, medium fat	30 mL (2 tbsp)
25 g	Sausage, Pork, Link	1 link
65 g	Spareribs or Shortribs, with bone	10 cm x 6 cm (4" x 2½")
25 g	Stewing Beef	1 cube, 25 mm (1")
25 g	Wiener	½ medium

Miscellaneous

15 g	Peanut Butter, all kinds	15 mL (1 tbsp)

Starchy Foods ◨

This group includes breads, cereals, grains, pasta, dried beans and peas, starchy vegetables and some prepared foods. Starch is a complex carbohydrate which gradually breaks down to sugar during digestion.

Some starchy foods are valuable sources of dietary fibers. These fibers are the portions of edible plants that are not digested by humans. Some of these fibers, such as those from dried peas and beans, delay carbohydrate absorption and thus slow the entry of sugar into the blood stream. Other fibers, such as cereal fibers, aid in elimination. A high-fiber diet also may help to promote weight loss by creating a feeling of fullness and satisfaction. To increase the fiber in your diet, try to choose more high-fiber foods such as dried beans, peas, lentils, whole grain breads and cereals.

One Choice from the Starchy Foods Group ◨ contains approximately 15 g starch (carbohydrate) and 2 g of protein and yields an energy value of about 290 kilojoules (68 Calories).

Breads

25 g	Bagel, Kaiser Roll	½
20 g	Bread Sticks, 11 cm x 1 cm (4½" x ½")	2
45 g	Brewis, cooked	50 mL (¼ cup)
25 g	English Muffin, Crumpet	½
30 g	Hamburger Bun, Hot Dog Bun	½
20 g	Matzoh, 15 cm (6" square)	1
15 g	Melba Toast, rectangular	4
25 g	Plain Roll	1 small
20 g	Rusks	2
25 g	Rye, coarse or Pumpernickel, 10 cm x 10 cm x 8 mm (4" x 4" x ⅜")	½ slice
20 g	Soda Crackers	8 small, 6 medium
25 g	Whole Wheat, Cracked Wheat, Rye, White Enriched	1 slice

Pastas

70 g	Macaroni — cooked	125 mL (½ cup)
80 g	Noodles — cooked	125 mL (½ cup)
70 g	Spaghetti — cooked	125 mL (½ cup)

Cereals

125 g	Cooked Cereals — cooked	125 mL (½ cup)
20 g	— dry	30 mL (2 tbsp)
125 g	Cornmeal — cooked	125 mL (½ cup)
20 g	— dry	30 mL (2 tbsp)
20 g	*Ready-to-Eat Unsweetened Cereal	125 mL (½ cup)
20 g	Shredded Wheat Biscuit, rectangular or round	1
30 g	Wheat Germ	75 mL (⅓ cup)

Grains

120 g	Barley — cooked	125 mL (½ cup)
20 g	— dry	30 mL (2 tbsp)
70 g	Bulgar, Kasha — cooked, moist	125 mL (½ cup)
40 g	— cooked, crumbly	75 mL (⅓ cup)
20 g	— dry	30 mL (2 tbsp)
70 g	Rice — cooked, loosely packed	125 mL (½ cup)
70 g	— cooked, tightly packed	75 mL (⅓ cup)

Starchy Vegetables

80 g	Beans & Peas (dried) — cooked	125 mL (½ cup)
85 g	Corn — canned, whole kernel	125 mL (½ cup)
60 g	— canned, creamed	75 mL (⅓ cup)
140 g	Corn, on the cob, 13 cm, 4 cm diameter (5″, 1½″ diameter)	1 small cob
20 g	Popcorn, unbuttered, large kernel	750 mL (3 cups)
105 g	Potatoes, whipped	125 mL (½ cup)
95 g	Potatoes, whole, 13 cm, 5 cm diameter (5″, 2″ diameter)	½
75 g	Yam, Sweet Potatoes 13 cm, 5 cm diameter (5″, 2″ diameter)	½

Cookies and Biscuits
See "Prepared Foods," following. For more detail refer to Convenience Foods, Canadian Diabetes Association.

*For more exact measures of various types of ready-to-eat cereals, see the cereals section of Convenience Foods which is available from the Canadian Diabetes Association.

Food items found in this category contain an additional 5 g fat and consequently an extra 190 kilojoules (45 Calories) = 1 ▲ Fats & Oils Choice.

Prepared Foods

30 g	Baking Powder Biscuit, 5 cm diameter (2″ diameter)	1
20 g	*Cookies, plain, (e.g. Digestive, Oatmeal)	2
35 g	Cup Cake, un-iced, 5 cm diameter (2″ diameter)	1 small
30 g	Doughnut, cake type, plain, 7 cm diameter (2¾″ diameter)	1
40 g	Muffin, plain, 6 cm diameter (2½″ diameter)	1 small
50 g	Pancake, homemade using 50 mL (¼ cup) batter	1 small
65 g	Potatoes, French Fried, 5 cm x 1 cm x 1 cm (2″ x ½″ x ½″)	10
260 g	*Soup, canned (Prepared with equal volume of water)	250 mL (1 cup)
35 g	Waffle, homemade using 50 mL (¼ cup) batter	1 small

*For more exact measures of various types of cookies and canned soups, see the appropriate section of Convenience Foods which is available from the Canadian Diabetes Association.

Milk ◆

This group includes milk and yogurt. Your dietitian will indicate the type of milk you should use in your *Eating Plan*.

Plain yogurt may be substituted for milk, but avoid sweetened yogurts which have a "fruit bottom" or added syrup. They contain extra sugar. Try making your own fruit-flavored yogurt by combining one Milk Choice as plain yogurt with one Fruits & Vegetables Choice. For a completely new taste, add bits of cut-up cucumber, green pepper and tomato to plain yogurt. Plain yogurt plus dill and other herbs such as thyme and parsley may be used as a tasty dressing for salads. You may use 25 mL (2 tbsp) of this mixture as an Extra ++ in your meal plan.

The *Milk Food Choices* are a valuable source of many nutrients — protein, calcium and phosphorous (needed for strong bones and teeth), thiamine and riboflavin. Since milk and plain yogurt are a source of carbohydrate (lactose or milk sugar) they are included in measured amounts in meal planning.

One Choice from the Milk Group ◆ contains approximately:

Skim Milk

6 g	Carbohydrate	170 kilojoules
4 g	Protein	(40 Calories)
0	Fat	

2% Milk

6 g	Carbohydrate	240 kilojoules
4 g	Protein	(58 Calories)
2 g	Fat	

Whole Milk

6 g	Carbohydrate	320 kilojoules
4 g	Protein	(76 Calories)
4 g	Fat	

125 g	Milk, Buttermilk	125 mL (½ cup)
50 g	Evaporated Milk	50 mL (¼ cup)
15 g	Powdered Milk, regular	30 mL (2 tbsp)
15 g	instant	50 mL (¼ cup)
125 g	Unflavored yogurt	125 mL (½ cup)

Fruits & Vegetables

This group includes fruits and many vegetables. Since certain vegetables such as corn and potatoes are high in starch, they are included in the Starchy Foods Group.

Fruits and vegetables are excellent sources of many vitamins and minerals as well as dietary fibers. Select a wide variety from this group for good health. Many fruits and vegetables (such as oranges, strawberries and turnips) are a valuable source of Vitamin C. Deep yellow fruits and dark green vegetables (such as peaches and winter squash) are usually high in Vitamin A.

Plan to have solid fruits and vegetables instead of juices. The natural sugar present in juice enters the blood rapidly, whereas the fiber content of solid fruits and vegetables slows the entry of sugar into the blood.

One Choice from the Fruits & Vegetables Group contains approximately 10 g of simple sugar (carbohydrate) and 1 g of protein, and yields an energy value of about 190 kilojoules (44 Calories).

Fruits
Fresh, frozen without sugar,
canned in water

75 g	Apple — raw	½ medium
120 g	— sauce	125 mL (½ cup)
115 g	Apricot — raw	2 medium
110 g	— canned, in water	4 halves, plus 30 mL (2 tbsp) liquid
75 g	Banana, 15 cm (6″), with peel	½ small
70 g	Blackberries — raw	125 mL (½ cup)
100 g	— canned, in water	125 mL (½ cup), includes 30 mL (2 tbsp) liquid
70 g	Blueberries, raw	125 mL (½ cup)
240 g	Cantaloupe, wedge with rind, 13 cm diameter (5″ diameter)	¼
160 g	cubed or diced	250 mL (1 cup)
75 g	Cherries — raw, with pits	10
90 g	— canned, in water, with pits	75 mL (⅓ cup), includes 30 mL (2 tbsp) liquid
120 g	Fruit Cocktail, canned, in water	125 mL (½ cup), includes 30 mL (2 tbsp) liquid
120 g	Fruit, mixed, cut-up	125 mL (½ cup)
185 g	Grapefruit — raw, with rind	½ small
100 g	— raw, sectioned	125 mL (½ cup)
120 g	— canned, in water	125 mL (½ cup), includes 30 mL (2 tbsp) liquid
75 g	Grapes — raw	125 mL (½ cup)
115 g	— canned, in water	75 mL (⅓ cup), includes 30 mL (2 tbsp) liquid
225 g	Honeydew Melon — raw, with rind	¹⁄₁₀
170 g	— cubed or diced	250 mL (1 cup)
100 g	Mandarin Oranges, canned, in water	125 mL (½ cup), includes 30 mL (2 tbsp) liquid
75 g	Nectarine	½ medium
130 g	Orange — raw, with rind	1 small

95 g	— raw, sectioned	125 mL (½ cup)
130 g	Peaches — raw, with seed and skin, 6 cm (2½") diameter	1 large
100 g	— raw, sliced, diced	125 mL (½ cup)
120 g	— canned, in water, halves or slices	125 mL (½ cup), includes 30 mL (2 tbsp) liquid
90 g	Pear — raw, with skin and core	½
90 g	— canned, in water, halves	2 halves, plus 30 mL (2 tbsp) liquid
75 g	Pineapple — raw	1 slice, 8 cm diameter, 2 cm thick (3¼" diameter, ¾" thick)
75 g	— raw, diced	125 mL (½ cup)
55 g	— canned, in juice, sliced	1 slice, plus 15 mL (1 tbsp) liquid
55 g	— canned, in juice, diced	75 mL (⅓ cup), includes 15 mL (1 tbsp) liquid
60 g	Plums — raw, prune type	2
100 g	— canned, in water	3, plus 30 mL (2 tbsp) liquid
70 g	— canned, in apple juice	2, plus 30 mL (2 tbsp) liquid
65 g	Raspberries, raw, black or red	125 mL (½ cup)
150 g	Strawberries, raw	250 mL (1 cup)
115 g	Tangerine — raw	1
100 g	— raw, sectioned	125 mL (½ cup)
310 g	Watermelon — raw with rind	1 wedge, 125 mm triangle, 22 mm thick (5" triangle, 1" thick)
160 g	— cubed or diced	250 mL (1 cup)
	Dried Fruit	
15 g	Dates, without pits	2
15 g	Prunes, raw, with pits	2
15 g	Raisins, Currants	30 mL (2 tbsp)

Juices
No sugar added or unsweetened

55 g	Apricot, Grape, Guava, Mango, Prune	50 mL (¼ cup)
80 g	Apple, Carrot, Pineapple	75 mL (⅓ cup)
130 g	Grapefruit, Orange	125 mL (½ cup)
255 g	Tomato, Tomato based mixed vegetables	250 mL (1 cup)

Vegetables
Fresh, frozen or canned

85 g	Beets, diced or sliced	125 mL (½ cup)
75 g	Carrots, diced	125 mL (½ cup)
80 g	Parsnips, mashed	125 mL (½ cup)
80 g	Peas — fresh or frozen	125 mL (½ cup)
55 g	— canned	75 mL (⅓ cup)
235 g	Sauerkraut	250 mL (1 cup)
100 g	Snowpeas	10 pods
115 g	Squash, yellow or winter, mashed	125 mL (½ cup)
240 g	Tomatoes, canned	250 mL (1 cup)
115 g	Turnip, mashed	125 mL (½ cup)
90 g	Vegetables, mixed	125 mL (½ cup)
50 g	Water Chestnuts	8 medium

Extra Vegetables ++

The vegetables in this group are low in natural sugar and energy value. However, they are high in dietary fibers, vitamins and minerals. Use them when you feel like nibbling. Moderate amounts of these vegetables do not have to be measured or calculated in your meal plan. Usually 125 mL (½ cup) cooked vegetables from this group contains less than 3.5 g of carbohydrate and yields an energy value of 60 kilojoules (14 Calories) or less. For some vegetables, 250 mL (1 cup) would be counted as one Fruits & Vegetables Choice ◢. These are indicated with an asterisk (*) in the following list.

Artichokes, Globe or French
Asparagus
Bamboo shoots
Beans, String, green or yellow
Bean Sprouts, Mung or Soy
Broccoli
*Brussels Sprouts

Cabbage
Cauliflower
Celery
Chard
Cucumber
*Eggplant
Endive
Kale
*Kohlrabi
*Leeks

Lettuce
Mushrooms
*Okra
Onions, green
*Onions, mature
Parsley
Pepper, green or red
Radish
*Rhubarb

Spinach
Sprouts: Alfalfa, Radish, etc.
*Tomato, raw
Vegetable Marrow
Watercress
Zucchini

Some vegetables are high in dietary fibre and low in available carbohydrate. They may be counted as ++Extra Vegetables if they are eaten in the portion size indicated with recipe, because only part of the carbohydrate is actually available to the blood sugar.

Fats & Oils ▲

This group includes a variety of high-fat foods such as vegetable oil, salad dressings, nuts, margarine and butter. All fats are a concentrated source of energy. Be especially careful to measure fats and oils if weight loss is necessary. If you have been advised to use polyunsaturated fats, choose oils such as safflower, sunflower, corn and soybean. Soft margarines in a tub with a label statement of "Polyunsaturated Fat 35%-55%, Saturated Fat 18%-25%" are recommended in preference to solid fats.

One Choice from the Fats and Oils Group ▲ contains approximately 5 g of fat and yields an energy value of about 190 kilojoules (45 Calories).

5 g	Bacon, side, crisp	1 slice
5 g	Butter, Margarine	5 mL (1 tsp)
30 g	Cream — Half and Half (cereal) 10%	30 mL (2 tbsp)
35 g	— Sour 12-14%	45 mL (3 tbsp)
15 g	Cream Cheese, Cheese Spread	15 mL (1 tbsp)
5 g	Lard, Salt Pork, raw or cooked	5 mL (1 tsp)
20 g	Nuts, shelled — Almonds	8 nuts
5 g	— Brazil Nuts	2 nuts
10 g	— Cashews, Filberts, Hazelnuts	5 nuts
10 g	— Peanuts	10 nuts
5 g	— Pecans	5 halves
10 g	— Walnuts	4 halves
5 g	Oil, cooking and salad	5 mL
15 g	Pâté, Liverwurst, Meat Spreads	15 mL (1 tbsp)
10 g	Salad Dressing — Blue, French, Italian	10 mL (2 tsp)
5 g	— Mayonnaise, Thousand Island	5 mL (1 tsp)

The **complete** *Good Health Eating Guide Food Groups* in color, and other information about diabetes, is available from the Canadian Diabetes Association. For a price list, contact your local Branch or Division, or the National Office, Canadian Diabetes Association, 78 Bond Street, Toronto, Ontario   M5B 2J8.

Reprinted by permission from CHOICE COOKING, 1983, Canadian Diabetes Association, published by NC Press, Toronto.

Notes

_____

_____

_____

_____

_____

_____

_____

_____

_____

_____

_____

_____

_____

_____

_____

_____

_____

_____

_____

_____

Appetizers and Small Snacks

Appetizers tease the taste buds and wake up the appetite for the rest of a meal. Many are tiny tidbits of food that can be eaten without forks or spoons. These are called "finger foods". They can be hot or cold and are often served in a casual manner in the living room or family room before dinner. Dips and vegetables, saucy meatballs or light soups, crisp salads, chilled juices and juicy fruit are also just right as the starter of a meal, and are usually served at the table. When the appetizer is the first course of a meal, it should be light and go with the foods that follow. For a snack party, serve an assortment of appetizers or bite-size foods.

From the variety I have included here, you can select dips and spreads, crisp breads and potato skins, hot meatballs and Falafel, plus Jelly Jubes.

When a small meal is what you fancy, and as long as it fits into your meal plan, one or two of these small snacks will fit the bill.

◀ From top clockwise:
Bunch of Crunch, Basil
Cheese Dip, Crispy Corn
Chips, Roasted Potato
Skins

Bunch of Crunch

On a tray or platter, set out an assortment of some or all of the following after the vegetables have been washed and trimmed: Whole green beans, broccoli and cauliflower florets, celery and sweet red and green pepper sticks, cucumber and zucchini slices, and red radishes.

Consider a handful of ++ Extra Vegetables. These are the right kind of vegetables to serve with a dip like Basil Cheese Dip (recipe, p. 47). All you will need to count is the Choice Value of the dip.

Keep in the refrigerator in plastic containers. Any or all of the vegetables are great for nibbling when you feel like an extra snack that is not included in your meal plan.

Each serving:
1 ++ Extra

Melba Toast

Preparation time: 5 minutes
Cooking time: 10 minutes

Call this "crisp bread" if you wish. It is like the melba toast served in top-notch restaurants and dining rooms. You may want to make up more than 4 slices at a time because the thoroughly dry, crisp triangles keep beautifully in a container with a loose fitting lid. They are great to have on hand to serve with soups and salads.

4	slices whole wheat bread	4

❶ Toast bread.
❷ Place each slice on a bread board. Cut off crusts and reserve for making bread crumbs. With a bread knife, holding the toast in place with the palm of the hand, carefully cut each slice in half horizontally to make 2 thin slices. Cut each thin slice in half, corner to corner, to form 2 triangles.
❸ Place triangles toasted side down on oven racks or nonstick cookie sheets.
❹ Bake in a 180°C (350°F) oven for 10 minutes or until triangles are dry and turn golden brown.

Makes 16 triangles, 4 servings

Each serving: 4 triangles (1 slice bread)
1 ☐ Starchy Choice

15 g carbohydrate   300 kilojoules
3 g protein   (72 Calories)

Mini Meatballs

Preparation time: 30 minutes
Cooking time: 10 minutes

It will take 20 to 30 minutes to make up these meatballs. You might like to plan a meatball making session as an evening or Saturday activity. Stash them away in the freezer where they will be ready and waiting to be cooked up for snacks, stews or in a sauce for spaghetti. Use them for Meatball Ragout (recipe, p. 111).

500 g	lean ground beef	1 lb
50 mL	fine dry bread crumbs	¼ cup
50 mL	water	¼ cup
25 mL	chopped fresh chives OR green onion	2 tbsp
5 mL	Dijon mustard	1 tsp
5 mL	Worcestershire sauce	1 tsp
2 mL	salt	½ tsp
1 mL	freshly ground pepper	¼ tsp

❶ In a large bowl, combine ground beef, bread crumbs, water, chives, mustard, Worcestershire sauce, salt and pepper. Mix well to blend flavors.
❷ With hands, roll 15 mL (1 tbsp) at a time into balls.
❸ Place on a broiler rack in broiler pan to allow fat to drain off.
❹ Bake in a 200°C (400°F) oven for 10 minutes or until lightly browned.

Makes 48 meatballs, 12 servings

Each serving: 4 meatballs
1 🖉 Protein Choice

2 g carbohydrate   260 kilojoules
7 g protein   (63 Calories)
3 g fat

● **Timely Tip:** Both uncooked and cooked meatballs freeze well. To freeze meatballs, place them in a single layer on a baking sheet. Place in freezer for 1 hour. (This prefreezing prevents balls from sticking together.) Remove and, working quickly, place in plastic bags, dividing into single serving-size portions or desired meal size. Close and fasten bags, pushing out all air. Remember to label with name, date and instructions for using. Immediately place in freezer. Store for up to 4 months. To cook frozen meatballs, place on rack in broiler pan and bake in a 200°C (400°F) oven for 15 to 20 minutes for raw meatballs, 10 to 12 minutes for precooked.

Potted Cheese

Preparation time: 5 minutes

This mildly sharp smoothy is so easy to make you will always want to keep a "pot" in your refrigerator.

250 mL	2% cottage cheese	1 cup
50 mL	shredded old Cheddar cheese	¼ cup
50 mL	cubed blue cheese	¼ cup
5 mL	Dijon mustard	1 tsp

❶ In a food processor or blender, combine cottage cheese, Cheddar cheese, blue cheese and mustard; process until smooth.
❷ Spoon into a small crock or dish.
❸ Cover and refrigerate until serving time. (Will keep up to 7 days in refrigerator.)

Makes 325 mL (1⅓ cups), 7 servings

Each serving: 45 mL (3 tbsp)

1 🖉 Protein Choice

1 g carbohydrate   230 kilojoules
6 g protein   (55 Calories)
3 g fat

Variations:

Potted Caraway Cheese: Add 5 mL (1 tsp) caraway seed to the above mixture.

Curried Potted Cheese: Use 5 mL (1 tsp) curry powder and 2 mL (½ tsp) bulk granulated sweetener, like SugarTwin, equivalent to 2 mL (½ tsp) sugar in place of the Dijon mustard in the above mixture.

Calculations as above

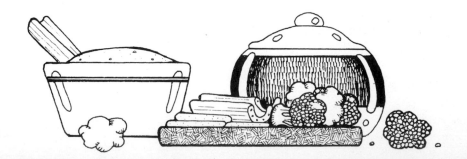

Cheese Chips

Preparation time: 5 minutes
Cooking time: 15 minutes

Not only are these crisp, cheesy crackers good on their own, they are excellent with soups or salads. Consider them for rounding out a meal.

125 mL	all-purpose flour	½ cup
125 mL	whole wheat flour	½ cup
125 mL	freshly grated Parmesan cheese	½ cup
2 mL	baking powder	½ tsp
Pinch	each white pepper, curry powder and salt	Pinch
25 mL	butter	2 tbsp
1	egg, lightly beaten	1
25 mL	water	2 tbsp

❶ Reserve 15 mL (1 tbsp) of the all-purpose flour for flouring board.
❷ In a bowl, combine remaining all-purpose flour, whole wheat flour, cheese, baking powder, pepper, curry and salt.
❸ With 2 knives, cut in butter until mixture resembles coarse crumbs.
❹ Combine egg and water; stir into flour mixture until mixture can be gathered into ball of dough.
❺ Knead dough on a lightly floured board 5 to 6 strokes. Roll out to 3 mm (⅛ in) thickness. Cut into 5 cm (2 in) triangles.
❻ Bake in a 180°C (350°F) oven for 12 to 15 minutes or until lightly browned.

Makes 36 chips, 6 servings

Each serving: 6 chips
1 ☑ Protein Choice
1 ☐ Starchy Choice

15 g carbohydrate   580 kilojoules
 6 g protein   (138 Calories)
 6 g fat

Cornmeal Tortillas (Cornmeal Pancakes)

Preparation time: 5 minutes
Standing time: 10 minutes
Cooking time: 15 minutes

Using cornmeal in this batter results in pancakes very similar to the Mexican tortilla. Crispy Corn Chips (see Variation below) can be made when the pancakes are cut up and dried out in a hot oven.

1	egg	1	
250 mL	water	1	cup
125 mL	all-purpose flour	½	cup
75 mL	cornmeal	⅓	cup
2 mL	baking powder	½	tsp
2 mL	salt	½	tsp

❶ In a bowl, combine egg and water. Stir in flour, cornmeal, baking powder and salt; beat well, then allow to stand for 5 to 10 minutes.
❷ Heat a nonstick frypan over medium heat. Brush very lightly with vegetable oil. Stir batter, then pour batter, 25 mL (2 tbsp) at a time, into frypan to make very thin pancakes.
❸ Cook until just dry on top. Do not turn. Stack until all pancakes are cooked. Stir batter as it is being used.

Makes 12 tortillas (pancakes), 6 servings

Each serving: 2 tortillas
1 ▣ Starchy Choice

13 g carbohydrate   310 kilojoules
3 g protein   (73 Calories)
1 g fat

Variation:

Crispy Corn Chips: Cut pancakes into 6 wedges. Lay wedges in single layers on nonstick baking sheets. Bake in a 190°C (375°F) oven for about 10 to 12 minutes or until lightly browned, crisp and dry. (Some pieces may be damper than others and may require a few more minutes baking.) Cool and pack into airtight bags.

Makes 72 corn chips, 6 servings

Each serving: 12 corn chips
Calculations as above

Roasted Potato Skins

Preparation time: 15 minutes
Baking time: 1 hour

*My kids and their friends love these snacks. They disappear be-
fore I can say "roasted potato skins". Fortunately the leftover
cooked pulp that I tuck in the refrigerator is excellent cold for
salad or rewarmed for the potato part of a meal.*

6	medium baking potatoes	6
5 mL	vegetable oil	1 tsp
10 mL	soft butter	2 tsp
	Garlic powder OR grated Parmesan cheese OR Salt and freshly ground pepper	

❶ Scrub potatoes. For each potato, place a few drops of oil in
palm of hand and rub it over the potato. Prick each potato with
a fork to allow steam to escape during baking.

❷ Place oiled potatoes on oven rack. Bake in a 200°C (400°F)
oven for 40 minutes or until tender.

❸ Remove from oven and cut each one in half crosswise. Let
cool until they can be handled. Scoop out potato pulp, leaving
about 3 mm (⅛ in) flesh clinging to skin. Cut each skin into 4
pieces. Reserve scooped-out potato pulp for dishes like Cheesy
Chive Potatoes (recipe, p. 156). If not using immediately, wrap
in plastic wrap and keep in refrigerator for up to 4 days.

❹ Dip a small pastry or paint brush into the soft butter. Brush
inside of each potato piece very sparingly with butter.

❺ Sprinkle very lightly with garlic powder or Parmesan or just
salt and pepper.

❻ Place potato pieces skin side down on nonstick baking
sheets. Bake in a 180°C (350°F) oven for 15 to 20 minutes or
until browned and crisp around edges.

❼ Serve hot or at room temperature. Store in covered container
or plastic bags in refrigerator if some of the potato pulp is still
moist, or in cupboard if skins and flesh are completely dry.

Makes 48 pieces, 6 servings

Each serving: 8 pieces
½ ▲ Fats & Oils Choice

2 g carbohydrate   130 kilojoules
1 g protein   (30 Calories)
2 g fat

Falafel

Preparation time: 10 minutes
Standing time: 1 hour
Cooking time: 15 minutes

In the Middle East, street vendors sell Pita Bread (recipe, p. 166) stuffed with Falafel and garnished with greens and yogurt. Try Falafel Patties in a hamburger bun to make a great vegetarian burger. Dress it with your favorite ++ *Extra relishes.*

1		can (540 mL/19 oz) chick peas, drained and rinsed	1	
50	mL	finely chopped celery	¼	cup
50	mL	finely chopped onion	¼	cup
15	mL	chopped fresh parsley OR 5 mL (1 tsp) dried	1	tbsp
1	mL	baking powder	¼	tsp
10	mL	sesame seed	2	tsp
1	mL	ground turmeric	¼	tsp
1	mL	ground cumin	¼	tsp
1		egg	1	
1		clove garlic, finely chopped	1	

❶ In a bowl, mash chick peas with back of large spoon or potato masher. Stir in celery, onion, parsley and baking powder; mix well. (Do not purée in blender or processor.)
❷ In a separate bowl, place sesame seed, turmeric, cumin, egg and garlic. Blend or whisk together until well blended. Pour into chick pea mixture; stir until well blended.
❸ Cover and let stand for 1 hour.
❹ With wet hands, shape into 2.5 cm (1 in) balls. Flatten slightly and place on lightly greased nonstick baking sheet. Bake in 180°C (350°F) oven for 15 minutes or until lightly browned. Serve warm with Nippy Yogurt Sauce (recipe, p. 87).

Makes 30 Falafel balls, 5 servings

Each serving: 6 Falafel balls

1 🖊 Protein Choice   16 g carbohydrate   500 kilojoules
1 ⬛ Starchy Choice   7 g protein   (119 Calories)
                         3 g fat

Variation:

Falafel Patties: Form Falafel mixture into 5 patties. Bake as for Falafel. Serve in pita pockets, remembering to count their Choice value.

Makes 5 patties, 5 servings

Each serving: 1 patty
Calculations as in basic recipe

Basil Cheese Dip

Preparation time: 5 minutes

Prepare and serve an assortment of crisp vegetables — celery, cucumber and zucchini sticks, broccoli and cauliflower florets, ivory mushrooms, ruby radishes — to use for dipping. Arrange them in cartwheel fashion around a bowl of dip set on a round plate or platter.

250 mL	2% cottage cheese	1 cup
50 mL	finely chopped fresh basil OR 15 mL (1 tbsp) dried	¼ cup
1	small clove garlic, crushed and chopped	1
25 mL	freshly grated Parmesan cheese	2 tbsp
2 mL	salt	½ tsp
Pinch	freshly ground pepper	Pinch

❶ In the container of food processor or blender combine cottage cheese, basil, garlic, Parmesan cheese, salt and pepper. Process for 1 to 2 minutes, stopping machine and scraping down side of container once or twice. (If machines are not available, with a wooden spoon, press cottage cheese through a sieve into a bowl; stir in remaining ingredients in order, making sure basil and garlic are very finely chopped).
❷ Transfer dip to a small dish.

Makes 250 mL (1 cup)

Each serving: 45 mL (3 tbsp)
1 ✪ Protein Choice

1 g carbohydrate   170 kilojoules
7 g protein   (41 Calories)
1 g fat

● **Helpful Hint:** Instead of 1 fresh garlic clove, you can use 2 mL (½ tsp) garlic powder for about the same flavor.

Fruit Jelly Jubes

Preparation time: 10 minutes
Standing time: 4 hours

For fruit jellies with a tasty, zingier flavor, use grapefruit juice in place of the orange juice; just be sure it is unsweetened.

5	envelopes unflavored gelatin	5
375 mL	unsweetened orange juice	1½ cups
10 mL	lemon juice	2 tsp
125 mL	bulk granulated artificial sweetener, like SugarTwin, equivalent to 125 mL (½ cup) sugar	½ cup
4	drops yellow food coloring	4
6	drops red food coloring	6

❶ In a small saucepan, sprinkle gelatin over orange juice; let stand for 5 minutes to soften.
❷ Heat over low heat just to simmering, stirring until gelatin dissolves. Remove from heat. Stir in lemon juice and sweetener.
❸ Pour into a 20 cm (8 in) square baking dish. Let stand for 4 hours at room temperature until firm.
❹ To remove from pan, cut around outside edges with sharp knife; place pan in shallow pan of hot water for about 30 seconds, just to soften bottom; loosen one corner, then quickly flip gel out onto a clean cutting surface.
❺ With a sharp knife, cut gel into 2 cm (¾ in) squares.
❻ Line a small box with waxed paper. Store gels in single layers with waxed paper between layers. Cover box and store in refrigerator.

Makes 100 squares, 25 servings

Each serving: 4 squares
1 **++** Extra

2 g carbohydrate   50 kilojoules
1 g protein   (12 Calories)

Variations:

Anise Jelly Jubes: Add 5 mL (1 tsp) oil of anise (available from the pharmacy in many drug stores) and about 20 drops of red food coloring.

Mint Jelly Jubes: Add 5 to 10 mL (1 to 2 tsp) peppermint flavoring and about 20 drops of green food coloring in place of yellow and red coloring.

Sour Jelly Jubes: Add an additional 10 to 15 mL (2 to 3 tsp) lemon juice and 10 to 15 drops yellow food coloring in place of red food coloring.

Grape Jelly Jubes: Use unsweetened grape juice in place of orange juice. No food coloring is required.

Calculations as in basic recipe

Cinnamon Toast

Preparation time: 5 minutes
Cooking time: 20 minutes

Keep triangles of cinnamon toast on hand as a light, crunchy snack for study or reading sessions. They keep well for at least a month in a tightly closed container.

4	slices whole wheat bread	**4**
25 mL	water	**2 tbsp**
	Artificial sweetener, like SugarTwin, equivalent to 30 mL (6 tsp) sugar	
	Cinnamon	

❶ Cut thin crust from each bread slice.
❷ Combine water and sweetener. With a brush, spread lightly on top of each slice of bread; sprinkle each with cinnamon.
❸ Cut each slice diagonally into quarters.
❹ Place triangles on nonstick baking sheet.
❺ Bake in a 180°C (350°F) oven for 10 minutes; turn bread triangles and continue baking 10 minutes longer or until lightly browned and crisp.

Makes 16 triangles, 4 servings

Each serving: 4 triangles
1 ☐ Starchy Choice

15 g carbohydrate   340 kilojoules
3 g protein   (81 Calories)
1 g fat

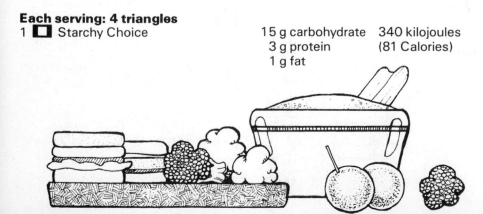

Recipe

Recipe	Food Choices Per Serving	Energy Per Serving kilojoules Calories		
Bunch of Crunch	1 ++ Extra Vegetables			p. 40
Melba Toast	1 ☐ Starchy	300	72	p. 40
Mini Meatballs	1 ⊘ Protein	260	63	p. 41
Potted Cheese	1 ⊘ Protein	230	55	p. 42
Potted Caraway Cheese	1 ⊘ Protein	230	55	p. 42
Curried Potted Cheese	1 ⊘ Protein	230	55	p. 42
Cheese Chips	1 ⊘ Protein; 1 ☐ Starchy	580	138	p. 43
Corn Tortillas	1 ☐ Starchy	310	73	p. 44
Crispy Corn Chips	1 ☐ Starchy	310	73	p. 44
Roasted Potato Skins	½ ▲ Fats & Oils	130	30	p. 45
Falafel	1 ⊘ Protein; 1 ☐ Starchy	500	119	p. 46
Falafel Patties	1 ⊘ Protein; 1 ☐ Starchy	500	119	p. 47
Basil Cheese Dip	1 ⊘ Protein	170	41	p. 47
Fruit Jelly Jubes	1 ++ Extra	50	12	p. 48
Anise Jelly Jubes	1 ++ Extra	50	12	p. 48
Mint Jelly Jubes	1 ++ Extra	50	12	p. 48
Sour Jelly Jubes	1 ++ Extra	50	12	p. 49
Grape Jelly Jubes	1 ++ Extra	50	12	p. 49
Cinnamon Toast	1 ☐ Starchy	340	81	p. 49

Notes

Hot and Cold Drinks

Frosty lemonade, frothy hot chocolate, steaming cider or creamy eggnog are all refreshing. Quick-to-fix beverages like these cheer you up, pick you up, cool you off or warm you up. They are wonderful to share with friends.

Keep the instant mixes on hand for quick-to-fix sodas and shakes. Some are energy-free and simply thirst quenchers. Others are more nutritious and yield energy indicated in the calculations, so make sure they fit into your meal plan before you make them.

Look through this section. You will find drinks for casual as well as more formal occasions, for kids and adults, for winter and summer. Have fun fixing them and drinking them!

◀ From top clockwise:
Lemonade, Frothy Rich
Hot Chocolate, Fruit Flip

Eggnog

Preparation time: 2 minutes

An eggnog makes a good breakfast in a hurry. This version is far less rich than the traditional one often served as a festive holiday treat.

1	egg		1
250 mL	skim milk		1 cup
5 mL	vanilla		1 tsp
	Artificial sweetener, like SugarTwin, equivalent to 5 mL (1 tsp) sugar		
Pinch	nutmeg		Pinch

❶ Combine egg, milk, vanilla and sweetener in a blender; process until smooth. (Alternatively, beat egg with whisk or hand beater, then beat in remaining ingredients.)
❷ Pour into glass and sprinkle lightly with nutmeg.

Makes 250 mL (1 cup), 1 serving

Each serving: 250 mL (1 cup) eggnog

1 ▨ Protein Choice	12 g carbohydrate	660 kilojoules
2 ◆ Milk Choices (2%)	14 g protein	(158 Calories)
	6 g fat	

Fruit Flip

Preparation time: 5 minutes

Not only is this flip a smooth, fruity snack that will pacify hunger pangs, it is also worth considering as a dessert.

175 mL	2% milk		⅔ cup
75 mL	2% yogurt		⅓ cup
1	small peach, peeled, pitted and sliced		1
5 mL	vanilla		1 tsp
	Artificial sweetener, like SugarTwin, equivalent to 10 mL (2 tsp) sugar		

❶ In container of blender or food processor, combine skim milk, yogurt, peach slices, vanilla and sweetener. Process until smooth. (Alternatively, in a bowl, mash peach until slushy. Stir in remaining ingredients; mix well.)

❷ Serve in a tall glass.

Makes 250 mL (1 cup), 1 serving

Each serving: 250 mL (1 cup)

1 ▨ Fruits & Vegetables Choice	22 g carbohydrate 600 kilojoules
2 ◆ Milk Choices (2%)	9 g protein (142 Calories)
	2 g fat

● Timely Tip: When fresh peaches are out of season, substitute a drained peach half, canned in juice or light syrup, for 1 fresh peach.

Spicy Mulled Cider

Preparation time: 5 minutes
Simmering time: 20 minutes

Mulled cider is a wonderfully warm, comforting brew that will make coping with a cold, blustery day a little easier.

500 mL	unsweetened apple cider or juice	2 cups
500 mL	weak tea	2 cups
5 mL	lemon juice	1 tsp
2 mL	whole allspice	½ tsp
2 mL	whole cloves	½ tsp
1	stick (5 cm/2 in) cinnamon	1
	Artificial sweetener, like SugarTwin, equivalent to 50 mL (¼ cup) sugar	
	Ground nutmeg	

❶ In a saucepan, combine cider, tea, lemon juice, allspice, cloves and cinnamon stick.

❷ Heat to boiling. Reduce heat, cover and simmer for 20 minutes to infuse the spices.

❸ Strain. Stir in sweetener. Taste; add a little more sweetener if desired.

❹ Serve in hot mugs. Sprinkle with nutmeg.

Makes 1 L (4 cups), 6 servings

Each serving: 175 mL (⅔ cup)

1 ▨ Fruits & Vegetables Choice	10 g carbohydrate 170 kilojoules
	(40 Calories)

Berry Essence

Preparation time: 5 minutes
Standing time: 8 to 9 hours

The vinegar draws out the "essence" of the berries and doesn't leave any vinegar aftertaste. Keep this concentrate on hand to make Berry Soda (recipe, p. 57).

375 mL	unsweetened fresh or frozen raspberries or blueberries	**1½ cups**
125 mL	water	**½ cup**
50 mL	vinegar	**¼ cup**
	Artificial sweetener, like SugarTwin	

❶ In a bowl or 1L (4 cup) measure, combine raspberries, water and vinegar.
❷ With a fork or back of a spoon, mash or bruise berries; stir well.
❸ Let stand at room temperature for 8 hours or overnight.
❹ Strain through a sieve into a clean bowl or measure, taking care not to mash or press berries to prevent pulp from mixing with juice. Allow to drip at least 30 minutes.
❺ Measure juice. To each 250 mL (1 cup) juice add artificial sweetener equivalent to 125 mL (½ cup) sugar; stir well.

Makes 250 mL (1 cup) concentrate, enough for 10 drinks

Each serving: 25 mL (2 tbsp) concentrate
½ 🔲 Fruits & Vegetables Choice   4 g carbohydrate   70 kilojoules
                                                                          (16 Calories)

Berry Soda

Preparation time: 2 minutes

If you keep different Berry Essences on hand, you will have the flavors for a variety of sodas.

200 mL	cold water or soda water	¾ cup
2	ice cubes	2
25 mL	Berry Essence (recipe, p. 56)	2 tbsp

❶ In a tall glass, combine water, ice cubes and Berry Essence; stir well. Serve.

Makes 200 mL (¾ cup), 1 serving

Each serving: 200 mL (¾ cup)

½ ▰ Fruits & Vegetables Choice	4 g carbohydrate	70 kilojoules (16 Calories)

Limeade

Preparation time: 2 minutes

Limes look like little green lemons, and seem to be available throughout the year. For a refreshing change, try a long, cool Limeade after exercising on a hot day.

250 mL	water	1 cup
25 mL	lime or lemon juice	2 tbsp
	Artificial sweetener, like SugarTwin equivalent to 15 mL (1 tbsp) sugar	
	Lime slice	

❶ Combine water, lime juice and sweetener.
❷ Pour over ice cubes in glass.
❸ Garnish with the lime slice.

Makes 250 mL (1 cup), 1 serving

Each serving: 250 mL (1 cup)

1 ✚✚ Extra	2 g carbohydrate	30 kilojoules (8 Calories)

Lemonade Syrup

Preparation time: 10 minutes

It's worth squeezing the lemons for this concentrate. Keep it bottled in the refrigerator as an instant mix for long refreshing coolers in summertime and for piping hot drinks in the winter.

	Thin outer yellow rind of 1 lemon	
250 mL	lemon juice (5 to 6 lemons)	1 cup
125 mL	water	½ cup
	Artificial sweetener, like SugarTwin, equivalent to 250 mL (1 cup) sugar	

❶ With a vegetable peeler or sharp knife, peel yellow rind from lemon in thin strips.
❷ In a saucepan, combine rind, juice and water; bring to a boil, reduce heat and simmer about 3 minutes.
❸ Cool, strain and stir in sweetener. Store in glass jar or bottle in refrigerator.

Makes 375 mL (1½ cups) concentrate, enough for 25 drinks

Each serving: 15 mL (1 tbsp) concentrate, enough for 250 mL (1 cup) lemonade
1 ++ Extra   1 g carbohydrate   20 kilojoules
                                                        (4 Calories)

Variations:

Lemon-Limeade Syrup: Replace 125 mL (½ cup) of the lemon juice with lime juice.

Lemonade Drinks:

Lemonade: For each glass of lemonade, combine 15 mL (1 tbsp) Lemonade Syrup with 250 mL (1 cup) ice water. Add an ice cube or two, if desired.

Hot Lemonade: Place 15 mL (1 tbsp) Lemonade Syrup in cup. Pour in 250 mL (1 cup) hot water.

Lemon Tea: For each cup, place 10 mL (2 tsp) Lemonade Syrup in tea cup. Pour over 200 mL (¾ cup) weak tea.

Iced Lemon Tea: For each glass, place 15 mL (1 tbsp) Lemonade Syrup in glass. Add 2 to 3 ice cubes and metal spoon. Pour weak tea over spoon. Stir. Add more ice, if desired. Garnish with thin lemon slice.

Calculations as above

Instant Chocolate Syrup

Preparation time: 10 minutes

Another versatile concentrate, this instant syrup is simple to make and easy to use. Keep it on hand to make Chocolate Banana Shake (recipe, p. 60), Chocolate Soda (recipe, p. 60) or Chocolate Cola (recipe, p. 61).

200 mL	dry unsweetened cocoa	¾	cup
Pinch	cinnamon		Pinch
300 mL	water	1¼	cup
5 mL	vanilla	1	tsp
	Artificial sweetener, like SugarTwin, equivalent to 125 mL (½ cup) sugar		

1 In a heavy saucepan, combine cocoa, cinnamon and water; stir or whisk until there are no dry lumps of cocoa. Stir and cook over medium heat until mixture comes to a boil. Reduce heat; boil gently, stirring often, for 5 minutes or until mixture is thick and smooth. Cool slightly. Stir in vanilla and sweetener.
2 Pour into a container or jar with lid. Cover and store in refrigerator for up to 3 weeks.

Makes 250 mL (1 cup) syrup

Each serving: 15 mL (1 tbsp)
1 **++** Extra

2 g carbohydrate   50 kilojoules
1 g protein   (12 Calories)

Chocolate Banana Shake

Preparation time: 2 minutes

The banana turns chocolate milk into a shake that's dairy bar thick, creamy and delicious.

½	small banana, cut in pieces	½
125 mL	skim milk	½ cup
10 mL	Instant Chocolate Syrup (recipe, p. 59)	2 tsp
1	ice cube	1

❶ In container of blender or food processor combine banana, skim milk, Instant Chocolate Syrup and ice cube. Process until banana is puréed and mixture is smooth. (Alternatively, in a bowl, mash banana. Stir in remaining ingredients; mix well.) Serve immediately.

Makes 250 mL (1 cup), 1 serving

Each serving: 250 mL (1 cup)
1 ◪ Fruits & Vegetables Choice   17 g carbohydrate   370 kilojoules
1 ◆ Milk Choice (skim)   5 g protein   (88 Calories)

Chocolate Soda

Preparation time: 2 minutes

This not-too-rich beverage is refreshingly bubbly chocolate milk.

125 mL	skim milk	½ cup
15 mL	Instant Chocolate Syrup (recipe, p. 59)	1 tbsp
3	ice cubes	3
75 mL	soda water	⅓ cup

❶ In a tall glass, combine milk and Instant Chocolate Syrup; mix well.
❷ Add ice cubes. Pour in soda and stir. Pop in a straw and serve.

Makes 200 mL (¾ cup), 1 serving

Each serving: 200 mL (¾ cup)
1 ◆ Milk Choice (skim)   8 g carbohydrate   220 kilojoules
                        5 g protein   (52 Calories)

Chocolate Cola

Preparation time: 2 minutes

When I was a teenager, this was all the rage. We'd order it at the café, where we would relax briefly after school.

1	can (300 mL) sugar-free cola	1
15 mL	Instant Chocolate Syrup (recipe, p. 59)	1 tbsp
	Ice cubes	

❶ In a tall glass, combine cola and Instant Chocolate Syrup.
❷ Add ice cubes and stir well. Serve with a straw.

Makes 300 mL (1¼ cups), 1 serving

Each serving: 300 mL (1¼ cups)
1 **++** Extra   2 g carbohydrate   50 kilojoules
                                 1 g protein   (12 Calories)

Frothy Rich Hot Chocolate

Preparation time: 3 minutes

Hot chocolate is on my list of "comfort foods". Is it on yours? The whisking creates a frothy top which I think is special.

200 mL	skim milk	¾ cup
25 mL	Instant Chocolate Syrup (recipe, p. 59)	2 tbsp
2 mL	vanilla	½ tsp
1	dollop whipped topping, optional	1
Pinch	ground cinnamon, optional	Pinch

❶ In a small saucepan, heat milk to simmering.
❷ Remove from heat; with a whisk, briskly beat in Instant Chocolate Syrup and vanilla.
❸ Pour into mug.
❹ Top with whipped topping and sprinkle with cinnamon, if desired.

Makes 200 mL (¾ cup), 1 serving

Each serving: 200 mL (¾ cup)
2 **◆** Milk Choices (skim)   13 g carbohydrate   350 kilojoules
                                 8 g protein   (84 Calories)

Recipe	Food Choices Per Serving	Energy Per Serving — kilojoules	Calories	
Eggnog	1 ⊘ Protein; 2 ◆ Milk (2%)	660	158	p. 54
Fruit Flip	1 ◗ Fruits & Vegetables; 2 ◆ Milk (2%)	600	142	p. 54
Spicy Mulled Cider	1 ◗ Fruits & Vegetables	170	40	p. 55
Berry Essence	½ ◗ Fruits & Vegetables	70	16	p. 56
Berry Soda	½ ◗ Fruits & Vegetables	70	16	p. 57
Limeade	1 ✚✚ Extra	30	8	p. 57
Lemonade Syrup	1 ✚✚ Extra	20	4	p. 58
Lemon-Limeade Syrup	1 ✚✚ Extra	20	4	p. 58
Lemonade	1 ✚✚ Extra	20	4	p. 58
Hot Lemonade	1 ✚✚ Extra	20	4	p. 58
Lemon Tea	1 ✚✚ Extra	20	4	p. 58
Iced Lemon Tea	1 ✚✚ Extra	20	4	p. 58
Instant Chocolate Syrup	1 ✚✚ Extra	50	12	p. 59
Chocolate Banana Shake	1 ◗ Fruits & Vegetables 1 ◆ Milk (skim);	370	88	p. 60
Chocolate Soda	1 ◆ Milk (skim)	220	52	p. 60
Chocolate Cola	1 ✚✚ Extra	50	12	p. 61
Frothy Rich Hot Chocolate	2 ◆ Milk (skim)	350	84	p. 61

Notes

Super Soups

Everyone loves a bowlful of soup. There is nothing like it — it's appetizing, comforting and satisfying.

Choose light, small servings, steaming or chilled, as a dinner starter, a planned snack between meals, or part of a salad and soup lunch. Or, make a heartier, stew-type soup or chowder for a meal-in-a-bowl — smooth or chunky, clear or creamy, hot or cold. My recipe collection includes all of these. Most of them are economical and easy to make.

Yes, one of the real joys of cooking is making soups. Once you have put all the ingredients in the pot and set it over the heat, enjoy the fragrant aroma as it brews and the flavors mingle. Soups look great with a simple garnish. Try a sprinkling of chopped parsley, green onions, or even paprika or curry powder.

Some vegetables are high in dietary fibre and low in available carbohydrate. They may be counted as ++ Extra Vegetables if they are eaten in the portion size indicated with the recipe, because only part of the stated carbohydrate is actually available as blood sugar.

◀ From top clockwise:
Curried Cucumber and
Tomato Soup, Broccoli
Soup, Onion Soup

Q and E Vegetable Soup

Preparation time: 5 minutes
Cooking time: 20 minutes

Q and E stands for quick and easy. It takes only 20 minutes for this soup to cook — just enough time to set the table and make a sandwich.

3	stalks celery, thinly sliced	3
2	medium potatoes, peeled and finely chopped	2
2	leeks OR 1 medium onion, thinly sliced	2
1	medium (15 cm/6 in) zucchini, cut in half lengthwise and sliced	1
250 mL	frozen green peas	1 cup
750 mL	chicken broth	3 cups
250 mL	shredded spinach OR leaf lettuce	1 cup
	Freshly ground pepper	

❶ In a large saucepan, combine celery, potatoes, leeks, zucchini and peas. Pour in broth.
❷ Bring to a boil, reduce heat and simmer for 15 minutes or until potatoes are tender.
❸ Stir in spinach and pepper to taste. Cook for 1 minute longer.
❹ Ladle into warm soup tureen or bowls.

Makes 1 L (4 cups), 4 servings

Each serving: 250 mL (1 cup)

1 ▢ Starchy Choice	26 g carbohydrate	520 kilojoules
1 ◪ Fruits & Vegetables Choice	5 g protein	(124 Calories)

Variations:

Creamy Vegetable Soup:

❶ Pour 125 mL (½ cup) milk in the container of blender or processor.
❷ Add 500 mL (2 cups) Q and E Vegetable Soup.
❸ Purée until smooth.
❹ Heat to serve or refrigerate and serve chilled.

Makes 625 mL (2½ cups), 4 servings

Each serving: 175 mL (⅔ cup)

1 ◆ Milk Choice (skim)	15 g carbohydrate	360 kilojoules
1 ◪ Fruits & Vegetables Choice	4 g protein	(85 Calories)
	1 g fat	

Cheesy Vegetable Soup:

❶ Pour Creamy Vegetable Soup into a saucepan.
❷ Heat, stirring, to simmering but do not boil.
❸ Remove from heat and quickly stir in 75 mL (⅓ cup) shredded Cheddar cheese or crumbled blue cheese; stir briskly, about 1 minute or until cheese melts.

Makes 625 mL (2½ cups), 4 servings

Each serving: 175 mL (⅔ cup)

1 ◆ Milk Choice (skim)	16 g carbohydrate	480 kilojoules
1 ◢ Fruits & Vegetables Choice	6 g protein	(115 Calories)
	3 g fat	

● **Helpful Hint:** Do not allow a soup or sauce to boil once cheese has been added. The only heat required is enough to melt the cheese when it is stirred briskly into a soup or sauce. Boiling causes the cheese to toughen and the sauce or soup to curdle.

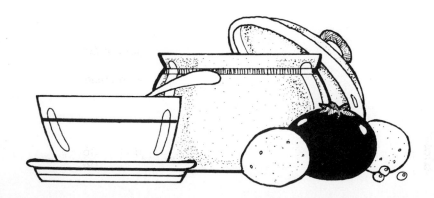

Bean Sprout Egg Drop Soup

Preparation time: 8 minutes

Adapted from an old Chinese recipe in my collection, this delicious soup rates as fast and fabulous. It is a soup with crunch since the bean sprouts barely cook.

750	mL	chicken or beef broth	3	cups
5	mL	soy sauce	1	tsp
10	mL	cold water	2	tsp
5	mL	cornstarch	1	tsp
250	mL	bean sprouts	1	cup
2		eggs, lightly beaten	2	
2		green onions, including green part, finely chopped	2	

❶ In a saucepan over high heat, bring broth to a boil.
❷ Combine soy sauce, cold water and cornstarch; stir again to mix well and stir into broth until it thickens slightly and is clear.
❸ Stir in the bean sprouts; bring mixture just back to a boil.
❹ While stirring, slowly pour in eggs and immediately take off heat.
❺ Ladle into warm tureen or individual bowls.
❻ Sprinkle with chopped onions and serve.

Makes 1 L (4 cups), 4 servings

Each serving: 250 mL (1 cup)

1 🖉 Protein Choice

3 g carbohydrate
5 g protein
3 g fat

250 kilojoules
(59 Calories)

Bacon and Bean Soup

Preparation time: 25 minutes

When the vegetables are finely chopped it takes only a short simmering time to develop and blend the flavors of the bacon and assorted winter vegetables. The beans add character and a heartiness that is satisfying. And an added plus — the soup is better a day or two after it is made. Store it in a covered container in the refrigerator.

3	slices back bacon	3	
3	stalks celery, chopped	3	
2	medium carrots, chopped	2	
1	medium onion, chopped	1	
250 mL	chopped turnip	1	cup
750 mL	beef broth	3	cups
1	bay leaf	1	
2 mL	dried thyme	½	tsp
1	can (540 mL/19 oz) kidney OR pinto beans, drained and rinsed	1	

❶ Cut bacon into thin slivers. In a 3 L (12 cup) saucepan, combine bacon, celery, carrots, onion, turnip, beef broth, bay leaf and thyme.
❷ Bring to a boil; reduce heat, cover and simmer for 15 minutes or until vegetables are tender.
❸ Add beans and continue to simmer 5 to 10 minutes or until hot, and flavors are blended.
❹ Remove the bay leaf and ladle into warm soup tureen or soup bowls.

Makes 1.5 L (6 cups), 8 servings

Each serving: 200 mL (¾ cup)
1 ☑ Protein Choice
1 ◻ Starchy Choice

15 g carbohydrate   450 kilojoules
7 g protein   (106 Calories)
2 g fat

Clamato Chowder

Preparation time: 10 minutes
Cooking time: 25-30 minutes

My son, Bob, hails this as "super" soup, and he is a seasoned food critic. Call it a soup-stew and make it a meal-in-a-bowl.

2	medium potatoes, peeled and chopped	2
1	medium onion, chopped	1
1	stalk celery, chopped	1
1	can (540 mL/19 oz) tomatoes	1
1	can (142 g/5 oz) clams	1
250 mL	water	1 cup
250 g	fresh or frozen fish fillets (cod, halibut, haddock or flounder)	½ lb
2 mL	salt	½ tsp
Dash	hot pepper sauce	Dash
15 mL	chopped fresh parsley	1 tbsp

❶ In a 3 L (12 cup) saucepan, combine potatoes, onion, celery, tomatoes, liquid from clams, (reserving clams for later), and water.

❷ Bring to a boil; reduce heat and simmer about 15 minutes or until potatoes are tender.

❸ Cut fish into bite-size pieces. Add clams, fish, salt and hot pepper sauce to potato mixture. Simmer for 10 minutes or until fish is opaque and flakes easily with a fork. (If cut up fish is still frozen or has ice crystals, add about 5 more minutes to cooking time).

❹ Ladle into warm tureen or soup bowls and sprinkle with parsley.

Makes 1.25 L (5 cups), 10 servings

Each serving: 125 mL (½ cup)

1 ☑ Protein Choice	8 g carbohydrate	380 kilojoules
½ ☐ Starchy Choice	8 g protein	(91 Calories)
	3 g fat	

Salmon Carrot Bisque

Preparation time: 7 minutes
Cooking time: 30 to 35 minutes

Classic bisques are usually thickened with a flour paste. Here the vegetables and salmon cook together for a soup light enough to start a meal or satisfying enough to make a main course when double portions are served.

1	medium potato, peeled and diced	1
1	carrot, diced	1
1	onion, chopped	1
1	stalk celery, diced	1
500 mL	chicken or fish broth	2 cups
1	can (106 g/3¾ oz) salmon	1
10 mL	lemon juice	2 tsp
2 mL	salt	½ tsp
2 mL	dried dillweed	½ tsp
Pinch	dried rosemary	Pinch
Pinch	freshly ground pepper	Pinch
25 mL	chopped fresh parsley, optional	2 tbsp

❶ In saucepan over medium heat, combine potato, carrot, onion and celery.
❷ Add broth; bring to a boil and cook, stirring, for 5 minutes.
❸ Stir in salmon, lemon juice, salt, dill, rosemary and pepper. Simmer for 20 minutes or until vegetables are tender.
❹ Add parsley if desired and simmer for 5 minutes.

Makes 1 L (4 cups), 4 servings

Each serving: 250 mL (1 cup)

1 ⊘ Protein Choice	7 g carbohydrate	350 kilojoules
½ ☐ Starchy Choice	7 g protein	(83 Calories)
	3 g fat	

Curried Cucumber and Tomato Soup

Preparation time: 10 minutes
Chilling time: 1 hour

This cool, crisp soup is best made in summer when the toma-
toes and cucumbers are in season, but make sure they are
peeled because their peel will be too bitter in this combination.

1		medium seedless English cucumber, peeled	1
1		medium ripe tomato, peeled	1
15	mL	chopped onion	1 tbsp
1		small clove garlic, chopped	1
1	mL	curry powder	¼ tsp
	Pinch	each nutmeg, salt and pepper	Pinch
125	mL	water	½ cup
15	mL	cider or wine vinegar	1 tbsp
2	to 4	drops hot pepper sauce	2 to 4
		Artificial sweetener, like SugarTwin equivalent to 10 mL (2 tsp) sugar	
		Chopped, fresh parsley, optional	

❶ Chop cucumber and tomato into medium-size chunks.
❷ In container of blender or food processor (fitted with metal blade), combine cucumber, tomato, onion, garlic, curry, nutmeg, salt, pepper, water, vinegar, hot pepper sauce and sweetener. Purée until smooth.
❸ Pour into a large bowl or pitcher. Chill at least 1 hour. Pour into soup bowls or mugs. Garnish with chopped parsley, if desired.

Makes 1 L (4 cups), 4 servings

Each serving: 250 mL (1 cup)
1 ++ Extra Vegetables   3 g carbohydrate   70 kilojoules
                                 1 g protein   (16 Calories)

Orange Tomato Bouillon

Preparation time: 3 minutes

To warm up the taste buds on a cold day, you can heat this made-in-a-minute soup. Hot or cold, it can also be served as a beverage.

250 mL	tomato juice	1	cup
125 mL	chicken broth	½	cup
125 mL	unsweetened orange juice	½	cup
5 mL	Worcestershire sauce	1	tsp
2 mL	soy sauce	½	tsp
2	drops hot pepper sauce	2	
	Grated orange rind, optional		

❶ In a pitcher or glass container, combine tomato juice, chicken broth, orange juice, Worcestershire, soy sauce and hot pepper sauce. Mix well.
❷ Pour over ice cubes in a wine glass or tumbler. Garnish with grated orange rind, if desired.

Makes 500 mL (2 cups), 2 servings

Each serving: 250 mL (1 cup)
1 ◈ Fruits & Vegetables Choice   12 g carbohydrate   240 kilojoules
                                         2 g protein   (56 Calories)

Broccoli Soup

Preparation time: 10 minutes
Cooking time: 30 minutes

This soup is also good chunky. If you prefer it chunky, just chop the vegetables a little finer than you need to when you're planning to purée them for a smoother soup. For a pale cream-colored soup, use cauliflower instead of broccoli.

1	bunch broccoli, chopped (1 L/4 cups)	1
1	medium potato, peeled and chopped	1
250 mL	chopped celery	1 cup
750 mL	water	3 cups
1	bay leaf	1
1	cube or packet instant chicken bouillon	1
2 mL	salt	½ tsp
Pinch	each nutmeg and white pepper	Pinch
	Paprika	

❶ In a large saucepan, combine broccoli, potato, celery, water, bay leaf, chicken bouillon cube and salt. Cover and bring to a boil. Reduce heat and simmer for 30 minutes.
❷ Remove bay leaf; transfer mixture to blender or processor fitted with metal blade. Add nutmeg and white pepper; process until smooth.
❸ To serve chilled or to store for later use, pour into bowl and refrigerate.
❹ To serve hot, return to saucepan; heat to simmering point.
❺ Ladle into soup bowls. Sprinkle lightly with paprika.

Makes 1 L (4 cups), 4 servings

Each serving: 250 mL (1 cup)
1 ◼ Fruits & Vegetables Choice

10 g carbohydrate   220 kilojoules
3 g protein   (52 Calories)

Onion Soup

Preparation time: 10 minutes
Cooking time: 1 hour

A hearty country-style soup, this pleasing combination of onions and cheese can be a meal in itself.

5 mL	corn oil	1 tsp
4	medium onions, thinly sliced	4
1	clove garlic, finely chopped	1
10 mL	all-purpose flour	2 tsp
1 L	beef broth	4 cups
2 mL	salt	½ tsp
Pinch	freshly ground pepper	Pinch
4	slices French loaf (1 cm/½ in thick)	4
75 mL	grated Parmesan cheese	⅓ cup
125 mL	shredded Swiss cheese	½ cup

❶ In 3 L (12 cup) Dutch oven or saucepan over medium high heat, heat oil. Add onions and garlic; cook, stirring occasionally, for 10 minutes or until onions are transparent and tender.
❷ Stir in flour and continue to cook, stirring, 10 minutes longer or until mixture turns brown without burning.
❸ Stir in broth, salt and pepper; cover pan and simmer for 25 minutes.
❹ Meanwhile, toast bread slices.
❺ On a jelly-roll pan, place 4 (375 mL/1½ cup) ovenproof bowls or small crocks.
❻ Ladle 250 mL (1 cup) soup into each bowl.
❼ Sprinkle 5 mL (1 tsp) of the Parmesan cheese over each bowl of soup, then top with a slice of toast. Sprinkle equal amounts of Swiss cheese over bread, then remaining Parmesan.
❽ Bake in a 180°C (350°F) oven for 20 minutes or until cheese melts and begins to brown. Serve immediately.

Makes 1 L (4 cups), 4 servings

Each serving: 1 bowl soup (250 mL/1 cup) and 1 slice of bread with cheese.

2 ▨ Protein Choices
1 ▧ Starchy Choice

18 g carbohydrate
14 g protein
8 g fat

840 kilojoules
(200 Calories)

Recipe	Food Choices Per Serving	Energy Per Serving		
		kilojoules	Calories	
Q and E Vegetable Soup	1 ☐ Starchy; 1 ◪ Fruits & Vegetables	520	124	p. 66
Creamy Vegetable Soup	1 ◆ Milk (skim); 1 ◪ Fruits & Vegetables	360	85	p. 66
Cheesy Vegetable Soup	1 ◆ Milk (skim); 1 ◪ Fruits & Vegetables	480	115	p. 67
Bean Sprout Egg Drop Soup	1 ⊘ Protein	250	59	p. 68
Bacon and Bean Soup	1 ⊘ Protein; 1 ☐ Starchy	450	106	p. 69
Clamato Chowder	1 ⊘ Protein; ½ ☐ Starchy	380	91	p. 70
Salmon Carrot Bisque	1 ⊘ Protein; ½ ☐ Starchy	350	83	p. 71
Curried Cucumber & Tomato Soup	1 ➕ Extra Vegetables	70	16	p. 72
Orange Tomato Bouillon	1 ◪ Fruits & Vegetables	240	56	p. 73
Broccoli Soup	1 ◪ Fruits & Vegetables	220	52	p. 74
Onion Soup	2 ⊘ Protein; 1 ☐ Starchy	840	200	p. 75

Notes

Zesty Salads

Salad-making brings out the artist in both beginning and experienced cooks. That's because almost anything edible can go into a salad — vegetables, fruits, meats, cheeses, eggs, pasta, rice, beans, nuts and seasonings. The combinations are determined by the creative flare of the salad-maker and the use of the completed salad.

Light salads make colorful appetizing starters for a meal or refreshing small courses with a meal. In my home, I often make and serve cold, hearty salads with protein in them as the main course, for brunch, lunch or dinner, especially in the hot summertime. A warm bread and a dessert usually round out the meal.

Summer salads are best because garden-fresh vegetables and orchard-fresh fruits are in season. However, crunchy salads such as coleslaw, carrot and zucchini put zest into winter meal planning and add excitement to meals.

Note: Some vegetables are high in dietary fibre and low in available carbohydrate. They may be counted as ++ Extra Vegetables if they are eaten in the portion size indicated with the recipe, because only part of the carbohydrate actually ends up as sugar in the blood.

◀ From top clockwise: Pork, Vegetables and Grapefruit in Lettuce Leaves, Chick Pea and Tomato Salad, Carrot and Zucchini Salad

Keeps-A-Week Coleslaw

Preparation time: 7 minutes
Chilling time: 1 hour

Here is a salad that is best if made in advance. It stays crisp for a whole week, covered, in a cold corner of the refrigerator. Spoon out servings, as required, and do try the innovative variations.

1.5 L	shredded cabbage (about ½ medium head)	6 cups
1	medium onion, finely chopped	1
1	medium carrot, shredded	1
	Artificial sweetener, like SugarTwin, equivalent to 50 mL (10 tsp)	
50 mL	vinegar	¼ cup
10 mL	vegetable oil	2 tsp
5 mL	Dijon mustard	1 tsp
2 mL	salt	½ tsp
2 mL	celery seed	½ tsp
2 mL	creamy horseradish	½ tsp
Pinch	freshly ground black pepper	Pinch

❶ In a large bowl, combine cabbage, onion and carrot.
❷ In a small saucepan, combine sweetener, vinegar, oil, mustard, salt, celery seed, horseradish and pepper. Heat to boiling.
❸ Pour hot dressing immediately over cabbage mixture. Stir well.
❹ Cover and chill for 1 hour, stirring occasionally, then serve or keep in the refrigerator for up to 7 days. At serving time, spoon into salad bowls or onto salad plates.

Makes 1 L (4 cups), 8 servings

Each serving: 125 mL (½ cup)
1 ➕ Extra Vegetables

3 g carbohydrate   110 kilojoules
1 g protein   (25 Calories)
1 g fat

See Note, p. 79

Variations:

Raisin Slaw: Into 500 mL (2 cups) Keeps-A-Week Coleslaw, stir 50 mL (¼ cup) chopped raisins or whole currants.

Makes 6 servings

Each serving: 125 mL (½ cup)

½  Fruits & Vegetables Choice

6 g carbohydrate	160 kilojoules
1 g protein	(37 Calories)
1 g fat	

Apple Yogurt Slaw: Into 500 mL (2 cups) Keeps-A-Week Coleslaw, stir 1 medium red apple, cored and chopped and 50 mL (¼ cup) 2% yogurt.

Makes 4 servings

Each serving: 175 mL (⅔ cup)

1 Fruits & Vegetables Choice

9 g carbohydrate	210 kilojoules
1 g protein	(49 Calories)
1 g fat	

Carrot and Zucchini Salad

Preparation time: 10 minutes
Chilling time: 20 minutes

Anyone counting calories will love this cool, colorful and crunchy salad.

2		medium carrots	2
2		medium zucchini (15 cm/6 in)	2
25	mL	orange juice	2 tbsp
15	mL	lemon juice	1 tbsp
		Artificial sweetener like SugarTwin, equivalent to 10 mL (2 tsp) sugar	
5	mL	poppy seed	1 tsp
	Pinch	each salt and freshly ground pepper	Pinch

❶ With a vegetable peeler, peel off and discard the rough outer skin of carrots. With vegetable peeler, continue paring the carrots into wafer-thin strips until as much of carrots as possible is used.

❷ With vegetable peeler, pare the zucchini into wafer-thin strips.

❸ Place carrot and zucchini strips in a bowl and cover with ice water; chill for 20 minutes.

❹ Drain vegetables well in a sieve or strainer. Transfer to a salad bowl.

❺ Combine orange juice, lemon juice, sweetener, poppy seed, salt and pepper. Pour over vegetables. Toss well.

❻ Serve.

Makes 500 mL (2 cups), 4 salad servings

Each serving: 125 mL (½ cup)

1 **++** Extra Vegetables

4 g carbohydrate   80 kilojoules
1 g protein   (20 Calories)

See Note, p. 79

Greek-Style Salad

Preparation time: 15 minutes

Feta cheese gives this salad a distinctive, salty, sharp burst of flavor.

½	medium head Romaine or iceberg lettuce	½
2	medium tomatoes	2
1	small cucumber	1
1	small red onion	1
125 mL	crumbled feta cheese OR cottage cheese (110 g)	½ cup
	Dressing:	
15 mL	olive oil	1 tbsp
15 mL	lemon juice	1 tbsp
5 mL	dried parsley OR 15 mL (1 tbsp) chopped fresh	1 tsp
2 mL	dried oregano	½ tsp
2 mL	garlic salt	½ tsp
Pinch	each thyme and freshly ground pepper	Pinch
6	pitted black olives, optional	6

❶ Tear lettuce into bite-size pieces. Cut tomatoes, cucumber, and onion into bite-size chunks.
❷ In a glass bowl, combine lettuce, tomatoes, cucumber, onion and cheese; cover and chill.
❸ Dressing: In a small bowl or cup, combine olive oil, lemon juice, parsley, oregano, garlic salt, thyme and pepper; beat together with fork or whisk.
❹ Pour dressing over salad; toss gently to coat ingredients with dressing.
❺ Slice olives; sprinkle over salad.

Makes 4 servings

Each serving: ¼ salad

1 ◆ Milk Choice (skim)
1 ✚✚ Extra Vegetables
1 ▲ Fats & Oils Choice

5 g carbohydrate   390 kilojoules
4 g protein   (94 Calories)
6 g fat

See Note, p. 79

Chick Pea and Tomato Salad

Preparation time: 10 minutes

For a complete protein meal, serve this hearty salad with grainy bread. Or try it tucked into Pita Bread (recipe, p. 166) for a superb sandwich.

1		can (540 mL/19 oz) chick peas or white kidney beans	1
2		medium tomatoes	2
25	mL	chopped chives OR green onion tops	2 tbsp
10	mL	vegetable oil	2 tsp
25	mL	malt vinegar	2 tbsp
5	mL	turmeric	1 tsp
5	mL	dillweed	1 tsp
2	mL	salt	½ tsp
	Pinch	freshly ground pepper	Pinch

❶ Drain and rinse beans, then drain well again. Place in a bowl.
❷ Peel tomatoes, if desired, and cut each tomato into 12 pieces. Remove seeds and place seeds in a sieve set over a bowl. Press to extract juice into bowl. Reserve juice.
❸ Add tomato pieces and chives to beans.
❹ Whisk oil, vinegar, turmeric, dillweed, salt and pepper into tomato juice. Pour over salad ingredients. Toss gently.

Makes 500 mL (2 cups), 4 servings

Each serving: 125 mL (½ cup)

1 ▨ Protein Choice	24 g carbohydrate	690 kilojoules
1 ☐ Starchy Choice	8 g protein	(164 Calories)
1 ◪ Fruits & Vegetables Choice	4 g fat	

Chicken Salad Chinois

Preparation time: 10 minutes
Chilling time: 2 hours

Chinois indicates a Chinese treatment, with the snappy flavor of ginger added to the finished dish — in this case an exciting cold chicken and vegetable combination.

500 mL	cut-up cooked chicken	2 cups
125 mL	chopped zucchini	½ cup
125 mL	chopped radishes	½ cup
50 mL	2% yogurt	¼ cup
15 mL	soy sauce	1 tbsp
2 mL	bulk granulated artificial sweetener, like SugarTwin, equivalent to 2 mL (½ tsp) sugar	½ tsp
2 mL	ground ginger	½ tsp
750 mL	shredded lettuce	3 cups

❶ In a bowl, combine chicken, zucchini and radishes.
❷ In a cup, combine yogurt, soy sauce, sweetener and ginger. Pour over chicken mixture; toss to coat evenly.
❸ Refrigerate at least 2 hours before serving, then toss well again.
❹ Place lettuce in salad bowl; spoon chicken mixture over; toss gently. Divide evenly into 4 portions.

Makes 1.25 mL (5 cups), 4 servings

Each serving: 300 mL (1¼ cups)
2 🍽 Protein Choices

2 g carbohydrate   550 kilojoules
15 g protein   (131 Calories)
7 g fat

Variation:

Chicken Salad in Pita Pockets: Cut 4 Pita Breads (recipe, p. 166), in half; open pockets and fill each pocket with one-eighth of Chicken Salad Chinois.

Makes 4 servings

Each serving: 2 Pita Pockets
[1 Pita plus 300 mL (1¼ cups) Chicken Salad Chinois]
2 🍽 Protein Choices
2 ⬛ Starchy Choices

33 g carbohydrate   1080 kilojoules
20 g protein   (257 Calories)
5 g fat

Pork, Vegetables and Grapefruit in Lettuce Leaves

Preparation time: 20 minutes
Cooking time: 20 minutes

The Vietnamese serve wonderful combinations of meats and vegetables and sometimes even noodles rolled up in lettuce leaves. What a neat way to eat a salad! No fork is needed.

500	g	boneless pork shoulder or loin, cut in 1 cm (½ in) slices	1 lb
250	mL	chicken broth	1 cup
10		fresh or defrosted medium shrimp, peeled and cleaned	10
1		small onion	1
1		medium carrot	1
½		seedless English cucumber	½
250	mL	bean sprouts	1 cup
1		small grapefruit	1
25	mL	toasted sesame seeds	2 tbsp
25	mL	soy sauce	2 tbsp
		Artificial sweetener, like SugarTwin, equivalent to 5 mL (1 tsp) sugar	
12		small lettuce leaves	12

❶ Trim pork of any visible fat.
❷ In a saucepan, combine pork and broth. Bring to a boil; reduce heat and simmer, uncovered, for 10 minutes.
❸ Add shrimp, cover and continue to simmer for 3 to 5 minutes longer or until pork is no longer pink and shrimp is cooked. Remove from heat and allow pork and shrimp to cool in liquid. Drain, then cut pork into thin strips and cut shrimp into slivers.
❹ Cut onion in half lengthwise, then into thin crosswise slices.
❺ Shred carrot and cucumber as for soleslaw. Squeeze out moisture.
❻ Wash bean sprouts, removing bitter root ends, and chop.
❼ In a bowl or on a platter, pile ingredients in separate mounds, cover and refrigerate.
❽ Before serving, cut grapefruit in half. Scoop out pulp, reserving shells. Remove pulp from membranes, discarding membranes and seeds. Add pulp to prepared vegetables and meat.

⑨ Sprinkle sesame seeds, soy sauce and sweetener over mixture. Toss thoroughly to coat ingredients with dressing.
⑩ Spoon into bowl or empty grapefruit shells, if desired, to serve. Place rinsed and dried lettuce leaves on plate. Have each diner spoon about 50 mL (¼ cup) salad onto a lettuce leaf, then fold in sides and roll up leaves to eat by hand.

Makes 750 mL (3 cups) filling, 6 servings

Each serving: 2 rolls (125 mL/½ cup mixture and 2 lettuce leaves)

2 ⬛ Protein Choices
½ ⬛ Fruits & Vegetables Choice

6 g carbohydrate   650 kilojoules
17 g protein   (155 Calories)
7 g fat

Nippy Yogurt Sauce

Preparation time: 2 minutes

What a versatile sauce! Use it as a dip for hot meatballs or crisp vegetables, as a relish for meaty hamburgers or tuna sandwiches, and as a dressing for crisp greens or sliced tomatoes.

125 mL	2% yogurt	½ cup
25 mL	sweet green relish	2 tbsp
	Artificial sweetener, like SugarTwin, equivalent to 1 mL (¼ tsp) sugar	
5 mL	curry powder	1 tsp

❶ In a small mixing bowl, combine yogurt, relish, sweetener and curry powder; mix well.

Makes 175 mL (⅔ cup)

Each serving: 15 mL (1 tbsp)

1 ➕ Extra

2 g carbohydrate   50 kilojoules
1 g protein   (12 Calories)

Tomato Sauce

Preparation time: 10 minutes
Cooking time: 30 to 45 minutes

For a rich, tomatoey sauce, I always use pulpy, plum tomatoes. This one keeps well, so it is smart to make it up ahead on an evening or Saturday set aside for cooking. Then all you have to do at mealtime is cook the pasta and heat the sauce, adding a few cooked meatballs, and a quick and tasty dish is ready. Complete the meal with a salad of crispy greens.

1	can (540 mL/19 oz) Italian plum tomatoes	1
1	packet or cube instant beef bouillon	1
2	cloves garlic, finely chopped	2
2	stalks celery, chopped	2
1	medium onion, chopped	1
½	green pepper, seeded and chopped	½
25 mL	chopped fresh parsley OR 10 mL (2 tsp) dried	2 tbsp
15 mL	chopped fresh basil OR 5 mL (1 tsp) dried	1 tbsp
2 mL	salt	½ tsp
2 mL	each thyme and oregano	½ tsp
Dash	hot pepper sauce	Dash

❶ In a saucepan, combine all ingredients. Stir, breaking up tomatoes.
❷ Bring to a boil; reduce heat and simmer for 30 to 45 minutes or until vegetables are tender. Purée if desired. Refrigerate or freeze.

Makes 375 mL (1½ cups)

Each serving: 25 mL (2 tbsp)
1 **✚✚** Extra

3 g carbohydrate   70 kilojoules
1 g protein   (16 Calories)

Each serving: 75 mL (⅓ cup)
1 **◼** Fruits & Vegetables Choice

10 g carbohydrate   200 kilojoules
2 g protein   (48 Calories)

● **Timely Tip:** Store tomato sauce in a covered jar or plastic container in the refrigerator for up to 10 days or freeze it for up to 4 months. Rememrber to label with name, date and instructions for use, just in case you forget what it is.

Tomato Tarragon Dressing

Preparation time: 5 minutes

This fat-free dressing is as good as commercial French dressings but without the fattening salad oil.

125 mL	canned tomato soup	½ cup
125 mL	tomato juice	½ cup
25 mL	wine vinegar	2 tbsp
25 mL	lemon juice	2 tbsp
15 mL	soy sauce	1 tbsp
15 mL	dried tarragon	1 tbsp
5 mL	Dijon mustard	1 tsp
1	clove garlic, mashed and chopped	1
	Artificial sweetener, like SugarTwin, equivalent to 10 mL (2 tsp) sugar	
2	drops hot pepper sauce	2

❶ In a blender, food processor or jar with screw-top lid, combine tomato soup, tomato juice, vinegar, lemon juice, soy sauce, tarragon, mustard, garlic, sweetener and hot pepper sauce.
❷ Process or shake for about 10 seconds.
❸ If processed, pour into jar with screw-top lid.
❹ Keep in refrigerator. Always shake before using.

Makes about 375 mL (1½ cups)

Each serving: 25 mL (2 tbsp)
1 **++** Extra   2 g carbohydrate   30 kilojoules
                                                       (8 Calories)

Recipe	Food Choices Per Serving	Energy Per Serving kilojoules Calories		
Keeps-A-Week Coleslaw	1 ✚✚ Extra Vegetables	110	25	p. 80
Raisin Slaw	½ ◪ Fruits & Vegetables	160	37	p. 81
Apple Yogurt Slaw	1 ◪ Fruits & Vegetables	210	49	p. 81
Carrot and Zucchini Salad	1 ✚✚ Extra Vegetables	80	20	p. 82
Greek-Style Salad	1 ◈ Milk (skim); 1 ✚✚ Extra Vegetables; 1 ▲ Fats & Oils	390	94	p. 83
Chick Pea and Tomato Salad	1 ◪ Protein; 1 ◻ Starchy; 1 ◪ Fruits & Vegetables	690	164	p. 84
Chicken Salad Chinois	2 ◪ Protein	550	131	p. 85
Chicken Salad in Pita Pockets	2 ◪ Protein; 2 ◻ Starchy	1080	257	p. 85
Pork, Vegetables & Grapefruit in Lettuce Leaves	2 ◪ Protein; ½ ◪ Fruits & Vegetables	650	155	p. 86
Nippy Yogurt Sauce	1 ✚✚ Extra	50	12	p. 87
Tomato Sauce — 25 mL (2 tbsp) — 75 mL (⅓ cup)	1 ✚✚ Extra 1 ◪ Fruits & Vegetables	70 200	16 48	p. 88
Tomato Tarragon Dressing	1 ✚✚ Extra	30	8	p. 88

Notes

Satisfying Snacks and Sandwiches

Burgers and pizzas are both in this section. Also, there are some surprises, like make-ahead Freezer French Toast.

The Topless Burger is just that. It is open-faced with no bun on top. Noon-time treats to eat at home or pack for lunch are planned to fit into the meal plans of young people with diabetes. Others are hot and hearty. They make great tasting supper specials, that are fast to fix. Many of them can be made ahead to store in the refrigerator or freezer.

Why not plan a session and make Freezer French Toast and Tuna Turnovers ahead and stash them in your freezer. Then you will have instant take-out at home. That is the ultimate in convenience.

Few sandwich recipes have been included because I am sure you know how to make a regular sandwich. When you do, make sure you count all the Food Choices of both the bread and the filling you choose.

◄ From top clockwise:
Pizza Quiche, Topless
B L T Burger, Sassy
Chicken Fingers

Tuna Melt

Preparation time: 15 minutes

Few can resist this combination and it is unbelievably easy to make. Call it fantastic and fast, if you like.

1	can (198 g/7 oz) chunk tuna rinsed and drained	1
25 g	mozzarella cheese, shredded	1 oz
125 mL	chopped celery	½ cup
25 mL	sweet pickle relish	1 tbsp
	Freshly ground pepper	
6	slices whole wheat bread	6

❶ In a bowl, combine tuna, mozzarella, celery and relish. Season with pepper to taste.
❷ Toast bread slices. Place on a baking sheet. Spread 125 mL (½ cup) tuna mixture on each slice.
❸ Bake in a 190°C (375°F) oven for 10 minutes or until cheese melts.
❹ Serve immediately. Cut in half for meal-size servings, in quarters or sixths for snack-size serving.

Makes 6 meal-size servings; 12 snack-size servings

Each meal-size serving: 1 slice

1 🖉 Protein Choice
1 ◻ Starchy Choice

16 g carbohydrate   590 kilojoules
10 g protein   (140 Calories)
 4 g fat

Each snack serving: ½ slice

½ 🖉 Protein Choice
½ ◻ Starchy Choice

8 g carbohydrate   290 kilojoules
5 g protein   (70 Calories)
2 g fat

Freezer French Toast

Preparation time: 20 minutes
Freezing time: 1 to 2 hours

When you make these ahead, you can slip slices of Freezer French Toast into the toaster for a slick, change-of-pace breakfast without the early morning fuss of making this popular favorite from scratch.

4	eggs	4
125 mL	2% milk	½ cup
8	slices whole wheat bread (day old is best)	8

❶ Lightly brush unsalted margarine or butter onto a 32 x 38 cm (10½ x 15½ in) jelly roll pan.
❷ In a bowl, beat together eggs and milk with a fork or whisk. Dip slices of bread into egg mixture, coating both sides.
❸ Lay in a single layer on prepared pan, squeezing close together if necessary to fit.
❹ Bake in a 190°C (375°F) oven for 15 minutes or until firm.
❺ Cut bread slices apart and remove from pan. Cool to room temperature.
❻ Place on foil-lined jelly roll pan or baking sheet. Place in freezer for 1 to 2 hours to freeze solid.
❼ Wrap slices in plastic wrap, foil or freezer wrap, placing 2 slice-size pieces of wrap between each slice, making it easy to remove one slice at a time from package once they are frozen.
❽ Wrap well and store in freezer for up to 2 months. (Remove number of slices required at one time; rewrap and return remainder to freezer.)
❾ At serving time, pop frozen French toast slices into toaster. Serve on warm plates with Cinnamon Pancake Syrup (recipe follows).

Makes 8 servings

Each serving: 1 slice

1 ∅ Protein Choice	16 g carbohydrate	500 kilojoules
1 ▪ Starchy Choice	7 g protein	(119 Calories)
	3 g fat	

Pizza Quiche

Preparation time: 10 minutes
Cooking time: 35 minutes

Enjoy the best of both; the flavor and texture of popular pizza toppings baked in a surprisingly good crustless quiche.

5 mL	margarine	1 tsp
50 mL	chopped onion	¼ cup
1	clove garlic, finely chopped	1
2	slices whole wheat bread	2
200 mL	skim milk	¾ cup
2	eggs	2
2	egg whites	2
5 mL	dried oregano	1 tsp
50 mL	catsup	¼ cup
125 mL	shredded mozzarella cheese (50g/2 oz)	½ cup
6	medium mushrooms, sliced	6
1	medium tomato, sliced	1
1	pepperette (thin pepperoni), sliced (about 25 g/2 oz)	1
½	small green pepper, cut in strips	½
	Freshly ground pepper	
50 mL	freshly grated Parmesan cheese	¼ cup

❶ In a small frypan, melt margarine. Add onion and garlic; cook for about 5 minutes or until soft.

❷ Break bread into small pieces and place in a bowl or container of food processor. Add milk, eggs and egg whites. Blend until bread is crumbly in mixture. Stir in oregano and sautéed onion and garlic.

❸ Pour into a lightly greased 23 cm (9 in) pie plate.

❹ Bake in a 180°C (350°F) oven for 25 minutes or until set.

❺ Remove from oven and spread with catsup. Sprinkle with mozzarella. Top with mushrooms, tomato, pepperette slices and green pepper strips. Sprinkle with pepper to taste and Parmesan cheese.

⑥ Return to oven and bake for 10 minutes or until mozzarella melts and Parmesan begins to brown.

⑦ Cut into 6 wedges to serve.

Makes 6 servings

Each serving: ⅙ of quiche

1 ◪ Protein Choice

½ ◻ Starchy Choice

1 ◈ Milk Choice (2%)

11 g carbohydrate   620 kilojoules

10 g protein   (147 Calories)

Cinnamon Pancake Syrup

Preparation time: 5 minutes

Any leftover syrup should be stored, covered, in the refrigerator for up to 10 days. For the second time around, it is best if it is reheated.

250 mL	cold water	1 cup
	Artificial sweetener, like SugarTwin, equivalent to 200 mL (¾ cup) sugar	
15 mL	cornstarch	1 tbsp
5 mL	ground cinnamon	1 tsp
Pinch	ground nutmeg	Pinch
5 mL	vinegar	1 tsp
5 mL	vanilla	1 tsp

❶ In a small saucepan, combine water, sweetener, cornstarch, cinnamon and nutmeg. Stir until smooth.

❷ Heat over medium heat, stirring, until mixture comes to a boil and thickens.

❸ Remove from heat; stir in vinegar and vanilla.

Makes about 250 mL (1 cup), 8 servings

One serving: 25 mL (2 tbsp)

1 ➕ Extra

2 g carbohydrate   30 kilojoules

(8 Calories)

Tuna Turnovers

Preparation time: 15 minutes
Baking time: 15 minutes

Here is a lunchtime, tea-time, anytime sandwich innovation for tuna lovers. The chilled version travels well in a lunch bag to be enjoyed at school or at the office.

1	can (106 g/3¾ oz) water-packed tuna	1
2	stalks celery, sliced	2
25 mL	chopped onion	2 tbsp
250 mL	chicken broth	1 cup
5 mL	prepared mustard	1 tsp
2 mL	curry powder	½ tsp
10 mL	2% yogurt	2 tsp
4	slices enriched white bread, crusts removed	4

❶ Drain tuna and place in bowl.
❷ In a saucepan, cook celery and onion in chicken broth for 15 minutes or until tender; mash or press through sieve or purée.
❸ Add purée mixture to tuna; mix in mustard, curry powder and yogurt. Mix well.
❹ Roll bread with a rolling pin until flattened.
❺ Place one-quarter of tuna mixture on one half of each slice of bread.
❻ Brush a little water along edges of bread. Fold in half diagonally, from corner to corner, so edges come together to form triangles. Press edges together with a fork to seal.
❼ Place on nonstick baking sheet.
❽ Bake in a 200°C (400°F) oven for 10 to 15 minutes or until lightly browned.

Makes 4 turnovers, 4 servings

Each serving: 1 turnover

1 ∅ Protein Choice   14 g carbohydrate   460 kilojoules
1 ☐ Starchy Choice   9 g protein   (110 Calories)
                          2 g fat

● **Timely Tip:** Freeze Tuna Turnovers, wrapped well with foil or plastic wrap. They keep up to 6 weeks in the freezer section of the refrigerator. Use for bag lunches. The turnover will defrost by lunchtime and at the same time keep other foods in the lunch bag cold.

Basic Burgers

Preparation time: 5 minutes
Cooking time: 8 to 10 minutes

Now you can cook your own quarter pounder exactly the way you want it. Using lean ground beef means top-notch quality with less fat and shrinkage.

500 g	lean ground beef	1 lb
15 mL	finely chopped onion	1 tbsp
15 mL	cold water	1 tbsp
10 mL	Worcestershire sauce	2 tsp
5 mL	liquid beef buillon concentrate	1 tsp
3	drops hot pepper sauce	3

❶ In a bowl, combine ground beef, onion, water, Worcestershire sauce, bouillon and hot pepper sauce; mix lIghtly.
❷ Divide into 4 equal portions, and shape each into a 2.5 cm (1 in) thick patty.
❸ Choose cooking method:
Broil: Place burgers on broiler rack lightly oiled or sprayed with nonstick spray, 7.5 cm (3 in) from heat and broil for 4 minutes; turn and cook for 2 to 3 minutes on other side or to desired degree of doneness.
Bake: Place burgers on rack in shallow roasting pan. Bake in 160°C (325°F) oven for 7 to 8 minutes or to desired degree of doneness.
Barbecue: Place burgers on a lightly oiled grill rack over medium-high heat, about 10 cm (4 in) from coals and grill for 4 minutes; turn and cook for 2 to 3 minutes on other side or to desired degree of doneness.
Pan-cook: Place burgers in a nonstick or heavy skillet and cook over medium heat for 4 minutes; turn and cook to desired degree of doneness.

Makes 4 burgers, 4 servings

Each serving: 1 burger
3 ⊘ Protein Choices

21 g protein
9 g fat

690 kilojoules
(165 Calories)

Topless B L T Burger

Preparation time: 5 minutes
Cooking time: 8 to 10 minutes

This open-faced burger, smothered in mushrooms and bacon, is attractive and tasty as a dinner burger.

1	recipe Basic Burgers (recipe, p. 99)	1	
5 mL	Dijon mustard	1	tsp
4	strips lean bacon, cut in pieces	4	
8	small mushrooms, sliced	8	
2	whole wheat hamburger buns	2	
4	lettuce leaves	4	
1	tomato, cut in 4 slices	1	
2	green onions, sliced	2	

❶ Stir Dijon mustard into Basic Burger Mix.
❷ Shape into 4 patties; cook using method of choice.
❸ Meanwhile, in a skillet, cook bacon for 2 to 3 minutes or until crisp. Pour off excess drippings. Add mushroom slices to pan; stir-cook about 3 minutes or until there is no moisture in pan.
❹ For each burger, place lettuce leaf on half of each hamburger bun; top with burger, tomato slice, mushroom mixture and garnish with green onion.
❺ Serve on plates with knife and fork for eating.

Makes 4 burgers, 4 servings

Each serving: 1 burger

3 ⊘ Protein Choices	17 g carbohydrate	1230 kilojoules
1 ☐ Starchy Choice	25 g protein	(294 Calories)
1 ▲ Fats & Oils Choice	14 g fat	

Sunshine Burger

Preparation time: 5 minutes
Cooking time: 8 to 10 minutes

Just looking at this burger combination will make you think of California sunshine!

1	recipe Basic Burgers (recipe, p. 99)	1
4	sesame burger buns	4
10 mL	butter or margarine	2 tsp
	Spinach or lettuce leaves	
250 mL	alfalfa sprouts	1 cup
125 mL	cottage cheese, mashed	½ cup
1	small navel orange, peeled & cut in 8 slices	1
10 mL	sunflower seeds	2 tsp

❶ Shape Basic Burgers into 4 patties and cook using method of choice.
❷ Split and toast hamburger buns; butter lightly.
❸ For each burger, place spinach leaf on bottom half of roll; top with burger.
❹ Top burger with sprouts, cottage cheese, 2 orange slices, a few sunflower seeds, and other half of roll.

Makes 4 burgers, 4 servings

Each serving: 1 burger
4 🚫 Protein Choices
2 ⬛ Starchy Choices

32 g carbohydrate   1530 kilojoules
30 g protein   (365 Calories)
13 g fat

Sassy Chicken Fingers

Preparation time: 15 minutes
Cooking time: 25 minutes

Hot, moist chicken baked in a crusty crumb makes finger-licking good eating when dipped in a cool, creamy sauce. The "heat" in the sauce will depend on the amount of freshly ground pepper used.

	Chicken Fingers:	
3	boneless and skinless chicken breasts, (375 g/¾ lb in total)	3
25 mL	2% yogurt	2 tbsp
12	soda crackers, crushed	12
5 mL	dried thyme	1 tsp
2 mL	dried marjoram	½ tsp
1 mL	curry powder	¼ tsp
	Salt	
	Sauce:	
125 mL	2% yogurt	½ cup
25 mL	catsup	2 tbsp
25 mL	finely chopped celery	2 tbsp
10 mL	soy sauce	2 tsp
2 mL	very finely chopped garlic, optional	½ tsp
	Freshly ground pepper	

❶ **Chicken Fingers:** Trim breasts of any visible fat. Cut each breast into 8 even strips.
❷ In a bowl, combine chicken strips and yogurt. Stir gently to coat each piece of chicken with yogurt.
❸ In a shallow dish or plate, combine cracker crumbs, thyme, marjoram and curry.
❹ With a fork, place each chicken strip in crumbs and roll to coat with crumbs.
❺ Place on a cake rack set in a baking pan or dish. Repeat with remaining chicken strips until all are coated and lined up in a single layer on rack.
❻ Bake in a 190°C (375°F) oven for 25 minutes or until crumbs are lightly browned and crisp. Remove from oven and sprinkle lightly with salt to taste.
❼ **Sauce:** Combine yogurt, catsup, celery, soy sauce, garlic, if desired, and pepper to taste. Serve as a dip for Chicken Fingers.

Makes 24 Fingers, 3 servings, 8 Fingers each

Each serving: 8 Fingers, 60 mL (4 tbsp) sauce

3 ⊘ Protein Choices

1 ◻ Starchy Choice

15 g carbohydrate   1000 kilojoules

22 g protein   (238 Calories)

10 g fat

Sloppy Joes

Preparation time: 5 minutes
Cooking time: 20 minutes

Depend on the good old Sloppy Joe when you want a meal-in-minutes. The beef bouillon adds an extra burst of meaty flavor to the sauce.

250 g	lean ground beef	½ lb
1	small onion, chopped	1
1	stalk celery, chopped	1
1	can (213 mL/7½ oz) tomato sauce OR 250 mL (1 cup) Tomato Sauce (recipe, p. 88)	1
1	packet or cube instant beef bouillon	1
2 mL	Worcestershire sauce	½ tsp
Pinch	freshly ground pepper	Pinch
2	hamburger buns, split and toasted	2

❶ In a skillet, combine ground beef, onion and celery. Stir-cook, breaking up meat, about 7 minutes or until beef begins to brown and onion is tender.

❷ Stir in tomato sauce, beef bouillon, Worcestershire sauce and pepper. Heat until mixture boils; cook, stirring, for 2 to 3 minutes longer or until mixture is thickened to spooning consistency.

❸ Place toasted bun halves on plates.

❹ Spoon 125 mL (½ cup) meat mixture over each. Serve immediately.

Makes 4 servings

Each serving: 125 mL (½ cup) meat mixture on ½ bun

2 ⊘ Protein Choices

1 ◻ Starchy Choice

1 ✚ Extra Vegetables

20 g carbohydrate   780 kilojoules

15 g protein   (185 Calories)

5 g fat

Mini Pizzas

Preparation time: 10 minutes
Cooking time: 15 minutes

Making pizza at home is lots of fun. The Tomato Sauce has all the special spices that make pizza taste wonderful, so plan to make it ahead so it's ready when you are in the mood for this fast food.

4	English muffins, split in half	4
200 mL	Tomato Sauce (recipe, p. 88)	¾ cup
125 g	lean back bacon	¼ lb
6	mushrooms, sliced	6
4	stuffed olives, thinly sliced	4
1	small onion, sliced	1
½	green pepper, seeded and sliced	½
125 g	mozzarella cheese, shredded	¼ lb
75 mL	freshly grated Parmesan cheese	⅓ cup

❶ On each muffin half, spread 25 mL (2 tbsp) tomato sauce.
❷ Top each with one-eighth of back bacon, mushrooms, olives, onion and green pepper. Sprinkle each with mozzarella and Parmesan cheese, dividing evenly.
❸ Place on nonstick baking sheet. Bake in 180°C (350°F) oven for 10 to 15 minutes or until cheese melts and begins to brown.
❹ Serve immediately.

Makes 8 Mini Pizzas, 8 servings

Each serving: 1 Mini Pizza

1 🖊 Protein Choice
1 ⬛ Starchy Choice
1 🔺 Fats & Oils Choice

18 g carbohydrate   740 kilojoules
10 g protein   (175 Calories)
 7 g fat

Pizzeria Pizza

Preparation time: 10 minutes, plus time to make the dough for the crust
Baking time: 25 minutes

This homemade pizza is tops and a real treat for teens.

1	Pizza Crust, (recipe, p. 169)	1
1	batch Tomato Sauce, (recipe, p. 88)	1
1	medium onion, sliced	1
1	small green or red sweet pepper, seeded and sliced	1
8	medium mushrooms, sliced	8
6	slices back bacon, cut in strips (100 g/4 oz)	6
250 mL	shredded mozzarella cheese (100 g/4 oz)	1 cup
45 mL	freshly grated Parmesan cheese	3 tbsp

❶ Knead dough just enough to press out large air bubbles. With a rolling pin, roll dough to make a 25 cm (10 in) circle. Stretch to fit a lightly oiled 30 cm (12 in) pizza pan.
❷ Spread Tomato Sauce evenly on the dough right to the edges.
❸ Spread onion, pepper, mushroom slices and bacon strips in layers over sauce.
❹ Sprinkle evenly with mozzarella and Parmesan cheeses.
❺ Bake in a 220°C (425°F) oven for 20 to 25 minutes or until lightly browned.
❻ Cut into wedges and serve.

Makes 8 servings

Each serving: ⅛ pizza

1 🖊 Protein Choice
1 ◻ Starchy Choice
1 ◪ Fruits & Vegetables Choice
½ ▲ Fats & Oils Choice

23 g carbohydrate   800 kilojoules
11 g protein   (190 Calories)
6 g fat

● **Helpful Hint:** Use a baking sheet or jelly roll pan, if you do not have a pizza pan and don't worry about having the pizza round. Instead, roll the dough into a 30 x 25 cm (12 x 10 in) rectangle, or one that almost fills the pan. Place on lightly oiled baking sheet; build up the edges slightly. Fill and bake as above.

Recipe	Food Choices Per Serving	Energy Per Serving kilojoules Calories	
Tuna Melt — 1 slice	1 ⊘Protein; 1 ◻Starchy	590	140	
— ½ slice	½ ⊘Protein; ½ ◻Starchy	290	70	p. 94
Freezer French Toast	1 ⊘Protein; 1 ◻Starchy	500	119	p. 95
Pizza Quiche	1 ⊘Protein; ½ ◻Starchy; 1 ◆Milk (2%)	620	147	p. 96
Cinnamon Pancake Syrup	1 ++Extra	30	8	p. 97
Tuna Turnovers	1 ⊘Protein; 1 ◻Starchy	460	110	p. 98
Basic Burgers	3 ⊘Protein	690	165	p. 99
Topless B L T Burger	3 ⊘Protein; 1 ◻Starchy; 1 ▲Fats & Oils	1230	294	p. 100
Sunshine Burger	4 ⊘Protein; 2 ◻Starchy	1530	365	p. 101
Sassy Chicken Fingers	3 ⊘Protein; 1 ◻Starchy	1000	238	p. 102
Sloppy Joes	2 ⊘Protein; 1 ◻Starchy; 1 ++Extra Vegetables	780	185	p. 103
Mini Pizzas	1 ⊘Protein; 1 ◻Starchy; 1 ▲Fats & Oils	740	175	p. 104
Pizzeria Pizza	1 ⊘Protein; 1 ◻Starchy; 1 ◖Fruits & Vegetables ½ ▲Fats & Oils	800	190	p. 105

Notes

Make it Meat, Poultry or Fish

When I grew up in Saskatchewan, we had chicken nearly every Sunday in our house. My mom's roast chicken, with its sage dressing, was the best and it still is. When we did not have chicken, it was roast pork or beef.

Roasting, of course, is not the only way to cook meat and poultry. You can braise, boil, poach, stir-braise, barbecue and stew it. There are so many ways, there is no reason to ever fry it and add extra fat to your diet.

Fish is just as versatile and makes good light eating when it is not cooked in a batter in hot fat.

Supermarkets today offer an amazing assortment of meat: beef, pork, lamb and veal cuts, and chicken from roasting birds to boned breasts. You will find roasts, chops, steaks, cutlets, stewing meat and ground meat packaged in amounts to cook up for a family or a single serving.

Fish, from both saltwater and fresh, can also be purchased whole, in steaks or fillets. Like meats and poultry, it is available all through the year, fresh, frozen, and smoked, cured and canned.

Meat, poultry and fish provide complete protein. They are also important sources of vitamins and minerals in the diet. Select lean cuts of meat, poultry and fish when you shop, trim off any visible fat before and after cooking, and drain or skim off any fat that collects during cooking. If you do, you will reduce the amount of food energy provided by these foods. This is especially important for weight watchers.

Because these protein-packed foods are often the most costly part of a meal, they should be handled and cooked with care. Following recipe directions closely will help you do this. You will notice that I recommend using a roast meat thermometer. It takes the guesswork out of deciding when roast meat is done.

In my recipes, the seasoning (herbs and spices) and vegetables (onions, celery and green pepper) may be varied a bit to suit you and your family's taste without changing the amount of Choices.

◀ From top clockwise: Pork and Ratatouille, Roast Chicken with Grandma's Bread Stuffing, Crisp Fish Sticks

Roast Beef

For the best roast beef, choose a tender cut of beef: rib, sirloin, eye of the round or rump (the least tender). Other cuts, which are less tender, are better cooked in moisture by braising or stewing. Select a lean roast that is compact and evenly shaped, untied or tied.

Roasts smaller than 1.5 kg (3 lbs) dry out when cooked and seem tough, so it is wise to select heavier cuts for roasting. Plan to have a roast when a group are dining together, or plan ahead to use any leftovers for sandwiches or in combination with other foods to make sure every bit of the meat is consumed. It is convenient to have cooked roast in the refrigerator or freezer. It makes a great start to a quick and easy meal.

❶ Arrange roast, fat side up, on a rack in a shallow roasting pan.

❷ Sprinkle or rub your choice of seasonings on the outside of roast: mustard, garlic, rosemary, marjoram, pepper, Worcestershire sauce, but no salt. Salt tends to draw juices from the meat as it cooks.

❸ Insert a meat thermometer into the thickest part of the meat, making sure the tip does not rest on bone or in fat. Using a thermometer to register internal temperature is the best way to check whether or not a roast is cooked to the desired degree of doneness.

❹ Roast uncovered, in a 160°C (325°F) oven until cooked to desired doneness.

Rare: 45 minutes/kg (20 minutes/lb)
Medium: 55 minutes/kg (25 minutes/lb)
Well-done: 65-75 minutes/kg (30 minutes/lb)

❺ Once roast is cooked, remove it from the oven and place it on a hot platter and allow it to stand in a warm place about 15 minutes. This allows some of the juice to be reabsorbed, firms the meat and makes carving easier.

A boneless roast yields 7 to 8 servings per kilogram (3 to 4 servings per pound)

Each serving: 75 g (3 oz) Lean Roast Beef
3 **⊘** Protein Choices   21 g protein   690 kilojoules
                                          9 g fat   (165 Calories)

Meatball Ragout

Preparation time: 8 minutes
Cooking time: 30 minutes

Some of the chick peas are mashed to act as a thickener for this simple and satisfying one-pot meal.

1	can (398 mL/14 oz) tomatoes	1
1	medium onion, chopped	1
2	cloves garlic, mashed and chopped	2
1	packet or cube instant beef bouillon	1
½	sweet green or red pepper, seeded and sliced	½
20	Mini Meatballs (recipe, p. 41), cooked	20
250 mL	cooked chick peas, drained and rinsed	1 cup

❶ In a large saucepan or skillet, combine tomatoes, onion, garlic and beef bouillon. Bring to a boil; cook, stirring occasionally, about 4 minutes or until onion is translucent.
❷ Stir in sweet pepper and Mini Meatballs. Bring mixture back to a boil; reduce heat and simmer for 5 minutes.
❸ With a fork, mash half the chick peas and add to meatball mixture. Stir in remaining chick peas.
❹ Simmer for 5 to 10 minutes longer to heat thoroughly and until liquid evaporates enough to make a stew-like consistency.
❺ Divide equally into 4 bowls or deep plates and serve.

Makes 4 servings

Each serving: ¼ Ragout
2 ⊘ Protein Choices
1 ▢ Starchy Choice

18 g carbohydrate   730 kilojoules
14 g protein   (173 Calories)
 5 g fat

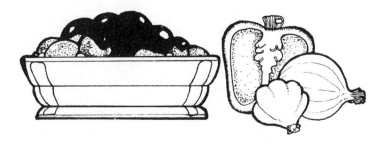

Sukiyaki

Preparation time: 15 minutes
Cooking time: 5 to 7 minutes

Legends tell us that early Japanese peasants were forbidden to eat meat. However, they did anyway by cooking whatever game they could catch right on the spot, on the metal of their hoes; suki means hoes, yaki means to broil. This dish is fun for entertaining because it can be cooked right at the table.

500	g	flank steak	1	lb
2		medium carrots, sliced	2	
1		medium onion, sliced OR 4 green onions, chopped	1	
6		medium mushrooms, sliced	6	
500	mL	shredded Chinese or regular cabbage	2	cups
250	g	snow peas OR green beans, trimmed	½	lb
250	g	bean sprouts	½	lb
125	mL	sliced bamboo shoots	½	cup
		Warishita: (Cooking Sauce)		
50	mL	soy sauce	¼	cup
50	mL	water	¼	cup
10	mL	red wine vinegar	2	tsp
5	mL	liquid beef bouillon concentrate	1	tsp
		Artificial sweetener, like SugarTwin, equivalent to 10 mL (1 tsp) sugar		

❶ Place steak in freezer for 1 hour before slicing. (It is much easier to slice if it is partially frozen.) Slice beef paper-thin across the grain.

❷ On a tray or platter, arrange beef and vegetables attractively in neat piles.

❸ **Warishita:** In a small pitcher or bowl, combine soy sauce, water, vinegar, bouillon concentrate and sweetener; reserve.

❹ Use electric nonstick skillet or put sukiyaki pan on table over heat.

❺ Pour about 50 mL (¼ cup) of the sauce into skillet; add slices of steak and cook at medium-high heat, stirring with spatula to cook slices quickly about 15 seconds on each side. Pour in a little more sauce and cook for 30 seconds longer, then move the steak to the side of the pan.

6 Add carrots and onion to pan; cook, stirring, for 2 minutes. Move them to another side of the pan. Add remaining vegetables and pour over remaining sauce. Stir-cook for 2 to 3 minutes longer.

7 Serve beef and vegetables separately from skillet or toss vegetables and meat together and serve.

Makes 4 servings

Each serving: ¼ of Sukiyaki (75 g/3 oz meat)

3 Ø Protein Choices	11 g carbohydrate	890 kilojoules
1 ∅ Fruits & Vegetables Choice	22 g protein	(213 Calories)
	9 g fat	

Variation:

Chicken Sukiyaki: Substitute chicken for the beef. Use 1 large whole chicken breast (500 g/1 lb) boned and skinned. (Also for ease in cutting, partially freeze the chicken for about 1 hour, then slice into fine thin pieces.) Use chicken bouillon instead of beef bouillon.

Makes 4 servings

Calculations as above

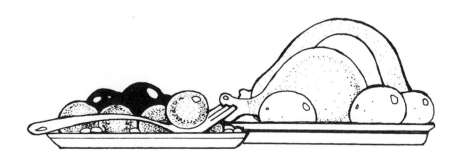

Pork Veronique

Preparation time: 10 minutes
Cooking time: 30 minutes

When the term "Veronique" is used, it means grapes are an ingredient in the finished dish.

250	mL	chicken broth	1	cup
500	g	pork tenderloin	1	lb
1		clove garlic, minced	1	
2	mL	dried thyme	½	tsp
250	mL	green seedless grapes, cut in half	1	cup
10	mL	cornstarch	2	tsp
15	mL	cold water	1	tbsp

❶ Into a shallow baking dish, pour broth.
❷ Cut tenderloin crosswise into 8 medallions or rounds and pound with a meat mallet gently until pieces are flat and round. Arrange in a single layer in broth. Sprinkle with garlic and thyme.
❸ Bake in a 180°C (350°F) oven for 15 minutes; add grapes and cook for 5 minutes longer. Transfer pork with slotted spoon to serving dish.
❹ Pour pan juices into small saucepan; bring to a boil and cook until reduced to half.
❺ Stir cornstarch into water; stir into pan juices. Stir and cook until thickened.
❻ Pour sauce over pork and grapes.

Makes 4 servings

Each serving: ¼ pork with sauce
3 ▨ Protein Choices
1 ▧ Fruits & Vegetables Choice

9 g carbohydrate   860 kilojoules
22 g protein   (205 Calories)
9 g fat

Pork and Ratatouille

Preparation time: 10 minutes
Cooking time: 30 minutes

Cooks throughout Southern France have their own special recipes for ratatouille. That strange word is the name for a glorious vegetable stew made with late summer vegetables: tomatoes, onions, zucchini and eggplant, the egg-shaped purple one. My version mixes in slivered pork for a complete skillet supper. You can use beef instead of pork, if desired.

500 g	lean pork shoulder or loin of pork, trimmed of all visible fat	1 lb
10 mL	soy sauce	2 tsp
	Artificial sweetener, like SugarTwin, equivalent to 5 mL (1 tsp) sugar	
5 mL	vinegar	1 tsp
500 g	eggplant, peeled and cubed	1 lb
1	medium onion, chopped	1
1	medium zucchini, sliced	1
1	clove garlic, finely chopped	1
5 mL	dried oregano	1 tsp
1	can (398 mL/14 oz) Italian tomatoes	1

❶ Cut pork into thin slivers, 5 x 1 x 1 cm (2 x ¾ x ¾ in).
❷ In a bowl, combine soy sauce, sweetener and vinegar; add pork and set aside to marinate.
❸ Meanwhile, in a skillet or large saucepan, combine eggplant, onion, zucchini, garlic, oregano and tomatoes; bring to a boil, stirring to break up tomatoes. Reduce heat and simmer, stirring occasionally, for 10 minutes.
❹ Stir in pork and marinade. Cook, stirring occasionally, about 20 minutes longer or until pork is no longer pink and excess moisture has evaporated.

Makes 4 servings

Each serving: ¼ Pork and Ratatouille

3 🥩 Protein Choices
1 🥬 Fruits & Vegetables Choice

12 g carbohydrate
21 g protein
9 g fat

890 kilojoules
(213 Calories)

Liver Creole

Preparation time: 15 minutes
Cooking time: 25 minutes

Liver is an excellent source of iron and should be included regularly in meal planning. Thin strips cooked quickly in tomato-green pepper sauce are always tender and full of flavor.

1	medium onion, chopped	1
1	small sweet green pepper, seeded and chopped	1
1	clove garlic, finely chopped	1
1	can (540 mL/19 oz) tomatoes	1
5 mL	dried basil	1 tsp
1 mL	ground cardamom	¼ tsp
Pinch	ground cumin	Pinch
5 mL	vegetable oil	1 tsp
500 g	beef or pork liver	1 lb
15 mL	red wine vinegar	1 tbsp
	Artificial sweetener, like SugarTwin, equivalent to 10 mL (2 tsp) sugar	
2 mL	salt	½ tsp
1 mL	freshly ground pepper	¼ tsp

❶ In a nonstick skillet, combine onion, green pepper and garlic; stir-cook for 2 to 3 minutes.
❷ Add tomatoes, basil, cardamom and cumin; simmer for 10 minutes.
❸ Brush separate skillet with oil. Sauté liver about 3 minutes on each side. Remove liver and cut into thin strips.
❹ Add liver strips, wine vinegar, sweetener, salt and pepper to tomato mixture; simmer for 3 to 4 minutes.

Makes 4 servings

Each serving: ¼ of creole
3 ⬛ Protein Choices
½ ⬛ Fruits & Vegetables Choice

7 g carbohydrate   880 kilojoules
23 g protein   (210 Calories)
10 g fat

Herb and Lemon Lamb Chops

Preparation time: 5 minutes
Marinating time: 2 hours
Cooking time: 15 to 20 minutes

The small amount of olive oil in the lemony, herb marinade is just enough to add flavor and help keep the chops from drying out when they cook.

4	shoulder lamb chops (500 g/1 lb total)	4	
	Juice of 1 lemon		
1	clove garlic, mashed and chopped	1	
15 mL	chopped fresh rosemary OR 5 mL (1 tsp) dried	1	tbsp
15 mL	chopped fresh summer savory OR 5 mL (1 tsp) dried	1	tbsp
5 mL	olive oil	1	tsp
Pinch	freshly ground pepper	Pinch	

❶ Trim visible fat from edges of chops. Discard trimmings. Place chops in a double plastic bag placed in a bowl.
❷ Combine lemon juice, garlic, rosemary, summer savory, olive oil and pepper. Pour over chops; close bag up tightly around chops with a wire twist-tie.
❸ Place in refrigerator to marinate at least 2 hours.
❹ Remove chops from marinade and pat dry with paper towels. Place on roasting rack or cake rack in a shallow pan.
❺ Bake in a 180°C (350°F) oven for 15 minutes for rare, 20 minutes for well done.

Makes 4 servings

Each serving: 1 lamb shoulder chop
2 🖉 Protein Choices

1 g carbohydrate
14 g protein
7 g fat

520 kilojoules
(123 Calories)

Chicken In A Package

Preparation time: 20 minutes
Baking time: 15 to 20 minutes

Food cooked in a foil or parchment packet actually steams in its own juices. The result is exciting and succulent. The flavor is fresh and the aroma fragrant.

1	medium carrot	1
1	medium (15 cm/6 in) zucchini	1
2	stalks celery	2
2	green onions	2
125 mL	thinly sliced mushrooms	½ cup
125 mL	chicken broth	½ cup
	Foil or cooking parchment paper	
2	whole chicken breasts (375 g/¾ lb total), split, boned and skinned	2
5 mL	dried summer savory	1 tsp
Pinch	freshly ground pepper	Pinch

❶ Wash and peel carrot. Wash and trim zucchini. Wash celery. Cut each vegetable into 5 cm (2 in) shoestring pieces (often called julienne cut). Cut onions lengthwise into thin strips 5 cm (2 in) long.

❷ In a skillet, combine carrot, zucchini, celery, onions and mushrooms with chicken broth. Stir-cook over medium heat for 2 to 3 minutes. Set aside to cool.

❸ Cut foil or cooking parchment paper into four 25 cm (10 in) squares.

❹ Place a half chicken breast diagonally near centre of each sheet. Top each with one-quarter of the braised vegetables and a pinch of summer savory and sprinkle of pepper. Fold other half of foil loosely over food to form a triangle. Fold edges together twice to seal securely. Place packages on a baking sheet. (Recipe can be prepared in advance to this point and refrigerated for up to 2 days.)

❺ Bake in a 160°C (325°F) oven for 15 minutes or until chicken is firm to the touch when pressed lightly with a finger. (To make this test for doneness, slit one package taking care not to spill juice, then press chicken.)

❻ To serve, slide each package onto a dinner plate, slit top and tear back foil to reveal chicken and vegetables. Slide out of foil package onto plate, if desired.

Makes 4 servings

Each serving: 1 piece chicken breast with about 125 mL (½ cup) vegetables

3 ⊘ Protein Choices

2 g carbohydrate   740 kilojoules
22 g protein   (177 Calories)
9 g fat

Grandma's Bread Stuffing

Preparation time: 15 minutes

My mom made stuffing like this for roast chicken and so did her mom, so it seems natural for me to use it regularly.

10 mL	margarine or butter	2 tsp
125 mL	chopped onion	½ cup
125 mL	chopped celery	½ cup
2 mL	dried sage	½ tsp
2 mL	dried summer savory	½ tsp
4	slices stale bread	4
125 mL	chicken broth	½ cup
Pinch	freshly ground pepper	Pinch

❶ In a medium saucepan, melt margarine. Add onion and celery; sauté about 5 minutes or until onion is translucent. Remove from heat.
❷ Stir in sage and savory.
❸ Cut bread into small cubes. Add to saucepan; toss with onion mixture.
❹ Sprinkle with chicken broth and mix until moistened. Season with pepper. Mix well.
❺ Stuff chicken, packing loosely because the stuffing will swell during cooking.

Makes 4 servings (enough for a 1.5 to 2 kg/3½ to 4½ lb chicken)

Each serving: 200 mL (¾ cup)

1 ☐ Starchy Choice
½ ▲ Fats & Oils Choice

17 g carbohydrate   390 kilojoules
2 g protein   (94 Calories)
2 g fat

● **Timely Tip:** Stuffed poultry (chicken, turkey, duck) should be roasted immediately after stuffing to prevent any chance of bacterial growth.

Lime-Broiled Chicken Breasts

Preparation time: 5 minutes
Marinating time: minimum 3 hours
Cooking time: 10 minutes

Marinating flavors the chicken. Plan so that the marinating is done ahead but leave the cooking until the last moment. Cook the chicken for the short time recommended, then serve it immediately. It is wonderful!

2	whole chicken breasts, boned, skinned and split (375 g/¾ lb total)	2
	Juice of 1 lime	
25 mL	soy sauce	2 tbsp
1	clove garlic, minced	1
15 mL	grated fresh ginger root	1 tbsp
	Artificial sweetener, like SugarTwin, equivalent to 5 mL (1 tsp) sugar	
	Salt and freshly ground pepper	

❶ Trim any visible fat from chicken breasts; place breasts in a glass bowl.
❷ Combine lime juice, soy sauce, garlic, ginger root and sweetener. Pour over chicken, coating each piece. Marinate in refrigerator, covered, for at least 3 hours or overnight.
❸ Preheat broiler.
❹ Remove chicken pieces from marinade and place pieces on broiler pan.
❺ Broil about 10 cm (4 in) from heat for 10 minutes, brushing with remaining marinade if surface seems dry.
❻ Season with salt and pepper to taste. Serve.

Makes 4 servings

Each serving: 1 chicken breast
3 🖊 Protein Choices

1 g carbohydrate   710 kilojoules
21 g protein   (169 Calories)
9 g fat

● **Helpful Hint:** To barbecue chicken breasts, first marinate them as directed above. Preheat barbecue, then place chicken pieces on the barbecue grill about 10 to 12 cm (4 to 5 in) over medium-high heat. Barbecue for 10 minutes, turning once and brushing with marinade. Overcooked chicken will be dry and seem stringy.

Roast Chicken

Preparation time: 15 minutes
Cooking time: 2 to 2½ hours (45 minutes per kg/20 minutes per lb)

For this first-class, old-fashioned specialty, buy Grade A roasting chickens. Stewing quality, utility birds become tough when cooked by the dry heat roasting method. Choose a firm ready-to-cook chicken for roasting.

1.5 kg	small roasting chicken	3½ lb

❶ Rinse and wipe chicken. Remove and discard any fat that can be pulled away from body cavity.

❷ Stuff bird, if desired. See Grandma's Bread Stuffing (recipe, p. 119).

a) Prepare stuffing. Do not stuff bird until ready to cook.

b) Fill neck cavity with dressing; pull neck skin over dressing to hold it. Secure flap of neck skin to back of bird with a skewer.

c) Stuff vent end (back end) of bird, taking care not to pack stuffing too tightly.

d) Skewer or sew the opening closed. (Use metal skewers or poultry pins or coarse thread on a darning needle.) If vent is too large to close, cover opening and exposed dressing with piece of foil.

e) Fold wing tips back under bird, then tie wings and legs close to body.

❸ Place bird breast side up on a rack in an open roasting pan.

❹ Brush skin with 1 or 2 drops of oil or margarine, if desired. (Do not add water to the pan.) Cover bird loosely with foil. Insert meat thermometer into thickest part of the thigh, not touching bone.

❺ Roast in a 160°C (325°F) oven about 2 to 2½ hours for a stuffed 1.5 kg (3½ lb) chicken. (If unstuffed, reduce roasting time slightly.) A half hour before cooking time is up, remove foil, and baste chicken with pan drippings to help brown.

❻ The chicken is cooked when internal temperature reaches 85°C (190°F), the leg joint moves when the drumstick is turned, the thickest part of the thigh feels tender and soft when pressed with a knife and juice runs clear and no longer pink.

❼ Place chicken on hot plate. Stand in a warm place for 15 to 20 minutes to allow juices to reabsorb and chicken to set. This makes the carving easier.

Makes 7 servings

Each serving: 75 g (3 oz) chicken, without stuffing

3 🖉 Protein Choices	21 g protein	690 kilojoules
	9 g fat	(165 Calories)

Chicken and Vegetable Stir-Fry

Preparation time: 10 minutes
Cooking time: 5 minutes

Chinese stir-fry cooking is certainly popular with busy cooks. It is no wonder! Fresh vegetables and cooked chicken go together for a nutritious meal-in-minutes. If you have cooked beef or pork on hand, use one or the other in place of the chicken.

125 mL	sliced carrots	½	cup
250 mL	unpeeled zucchini slices	1	cup
250 mL	diagonally cut celery slices	1	cup
1	medium onion, cut in half and sliced	1	
15 mL	corn oil	1	tbsp
1	clove garlic, mashed and chopped OR 2 mL (½ tsp) garlic powder	1	
125 mL	cold water	½	cup
15 mL	soy sauce	1	tbsp
10 mL	cornstarch	2	tsp
1 mL	ground ginger	¼	tsp
250 mL	cut-up cooked chicken	1	cup

❶ Prepare carrots, zucchini, celery and onion; set aside.
❷ In wok or large skillet (electric one is perfect), heat oil; add garlic and cook about 30 seconds.
❸ Stir in vegetables in order listed; stir-fry over medium-high heat about 3 minutes.
❹ Stir in water; reduce heat, cover and steam vegetables for about 7 minutes or until tender-crisp.
❺ In a small dish, blend together soy sauce, cornstarch and ginger. Push vegetables to one side of pan. Stir cornstarch mixture into broth in pan and cook for about 1 minute or until mixture thickens.
❻ Add cooked chicken. Gently stir together vegetables, thickened broth and chicken until chicken is heated through.

Makes 4 servings

Each serving: ¼ vegetables and chicken

1 ☑ Protein Choice	5 g carbohydrate	430 kilojoules
½ ▲ Fats & Oils Choice	7 g protein	(102 Calories)
1 ➕ Extra Vegetables	6 g fat	

Note: Only part of the stated carbohydrate from the vegetables is actually available to affect the blood sugar. This has been considered in assigning the Food Choice Value.

Stir-Braised Scallops with Vegetables

Preparation time: 15 minutes
Cooking time: 15 minutes

Pearly white, tender, scallops are low in fat, making the energy (kilojoules/Calorie) value of each serving low.

2	medium carrots, cut in julienne	2
500 mL	broccoli florets	2 cups
1	green pepper, chopped	1
1	clove garlic, finely chopped	1
125 mL	chicken broth	½ cup
2	green onions, chopped	2
250 mL	shredded cabbage	1 cup
250 mL	bean sprouts	1 cup
1	pkg (396 g/14 oz) frozen scallops, defrosted and cut in half crosswise	1
75 mL	water	⅓ cup
15 mL	soy sauce	1 tbsp
	Artificial sweetener, like SugarTwin, equivalent to 10 mL (2 tsp) sugar	
10 mL	cornstarch	2 tsp
25 mL	sliced almonds, toasted (8 almonds/20 g)	2 tbsp

❶ In a large skillet, combine carrots, broccoli, green pepper, garlic and broth. Stir-braise vegetables for 3 minutes.
❷ Add green onions, cabbage, bean sprouts and scallops; stir-cook for 5 minutes longer.
❸ Stir together water, soy sauce, sweetener and cornstarch; add to vegetables and scallops. Stir-cook about 3 minutes or until sauce thickens. Garnish with almonds and serve.

Makes 4 servings

Each serving: 250 mL (1 cup)
3 🥩 Protein Choices   9 g carbohydrate   610 kilojoules
½ 🥦 Fruits & Vegetables Choice   23 g protein   (146 Calories)
                                   2 g fat

Foil-Baked Lemon Fish Fillets

Preparation time: 10 minutes
Cooking time: 25 minutes

Fish is easy to cook. It does not take long because it is tender and has very little connective tissue. One caution I must mention; please watch the cooking time, and do not overcook fish. Overcooking causes flavor and moisture loss and also toughens fish. Perfectly cooked fish is opaque throughout, still springy when touched, and flakes easily when tested with a fork. For this recipe, use cod, flounder, haddock, halibut, Boston blue fish, salmon or sole.

2	squares (30 cm/12 in) heavy foil	2
10 mL	margarine	2 tsp
250 g	fresh or frozen (thawed) fish fillets	½ lb
25 mL	finely chopped celery	2 tbsp
10 mL	finely chopped onion	2 tsp
2	thin slices lemon OR 10 mL (2 tsp) lemon juice	2
Pinch	each salt and pepper	Pinch

❶ Lay foil on work surface, dull side up. Brush 5 mL (1 tsp) margarine over each piece of foil, leaving 5 cm (2 in) border around all sides free of margarine. Pressing gently, fold each square in half, diagonally from corner to corner, to form a triangle, then open up pieces of foil again.
❷ Divide fish evenly into 2 portions and place one portion on each piece of foil to one side of the fold line.
❸ Top each portion of fish with half the celery, half the onion and 1 slice lemon. Season with salt and pepper.
❹ Fold half of foil diagonally over fish and vegetables so that the two opposite edges and corners meet and form a triangle. Fold edges together twice and pinch to seal edges. Place packages on a baking sheet.
❺ Bake in a 200°C (400°F) oven for 25 minutes or until fish is springy when touched and flakes easily with a fork.
❻ To serve, place packages on dinner plate, cut an X through top of each package and eat fish right from the package, or transfer it with the juice to the plate.

Makes 2 servings

Each serving: 90 g (3 to 4 oz)

3 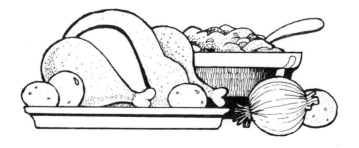 Protein Choices   24 g protein   740 kilojoules
                                                          9 g fat   (177 Calories)

Variation:

Foil-Baked Tomato Fish Fillets: In place of lemon slices, use tomato slices, cut 1 cm (½ in) thick.

Calculations as above

● **Timely Tip:** The foil-baked fish can be chilled in the refrigerator in its wrapping where it will keep up to 3 days. It is wonderful served cold with salads. And, if you can keep it cold, it makes a good totable lunch dish.

● **Helpful Hint:** Fish steaks can be used in the above recipes in place of the fillets. Buy 2 slices of fish 2 cm (¾ in) thick, 300 g (10 oz) total.

Crisp Fish Sticks

Preparation time: 10 minutes
Baking time: 12 minutes

These are better than the packaged frozen ready-to-heat ones and have very little added fat. To test fish for doneness, use a fork and pull the middle part of the fish gently; if it flakes easily, the fish is done.

500 g	fish fillets (flounder, whitefish, haddock, cod), fresh or frozen (thawed)	**1 lb**
125 mL	2% yogurt or milk	**½ cup**
5 mL	Worcestershire sauce	**1 tsp**
5 mL	soy sauce	**1 tsp**
12	soda crackers, finely crushed	**12**
250 mL	cornflakes, crushed	**1 cup**
Pinch	freshly ground pepper	**Pinch**
10 mL	margarine, melted OR corn oil	**2 tsp**
	Salt, optional	

❶ Cut fish into 8 even pieces (about 60 g/2 oz each).
❷ In a shallow dish or pie plate, combine yogurt, Worcestershire and soy sauce.
❸ In a second shallow dish or pie plate, combine crushed cracker, corn flake crumbs and pepper. With fingers, rub margarine into crumbs until evenly distributed.
❹ Dip each piece of fish into yogurt mixture, then into crumbs to coat completely. (If milk is used, you might have to dip fish twice: first into milk, then crumbs, then milk again and crumbs again.)
❺ Place fish 2.5 cm (1 in) apart on nonstick or lightly greased baking sheets. (Pieces should not touch.)
❻ Bake in 225°C (450°F) oven for 6 minutes; turn and bake for 5 to 6 minutes longer or until crumb coating is crisp and fish flakes easily when tested with a fork. Salt lightly after baking, if desired.

Makes 4 servings, 2 pieces 100 g (4 oz) per serving

Each serving: 2 fish fillets

4 ✅ Protein Choices
1 ⬜ Starchy Choice

14 g carbohydrate
27 g protein
  9 g fat

1030 kilojoules
(245 Calories)

Variation:

Dilly Crisp Fish Sticks: Add 5 mL (1 tsp) dried dill to crumb mixture in the above recipe.

Calculations as above

Baked Fish Fillets with Walnuts

Preparation time: 3 minutes
Cooking time: 12 minutes

The growing popularity of fish and seafood is not surprising. Both cook quickly and go well with many different flavors.

500 g	fish fillets (cod, flounder, haddock or sole), fresh or frozen (thawed)	1	lb
1 mL	salt	¼	tsp
Pinch	freshly ground pepper		Pinch
20 mL	chopped walnuts	4	tsp
4	lemon wedges	4	

❶ In a nonstick baking dish, place fillets in a single layer. Sprinkle evenly with salt, pepper and walnuts (5 mL/1 tsp per 125 g/¼ lb fillet).
❷ Bake, uncovered, in a 200°C (400°F) oven, basting once or twice, for 12 minutes or just until fish is opaque and flakes easily when tested with a fork.
❸ Serve on warm plates. Garnish each serving with a wedge of lemon.

Makes 4 servings

Each serving: 75 g (3 oz)
3 🖉 Protein Choices   24 g protein   670 kilojoules
                         7 g fat   (159 Calories)

Variation:

Baked Fish Fillets Parmesan: In place of walnuts, sprinkle 20 mL (4 tsp) grated Parmesan cheese evenly over fish fillets before baking.

3 🖉 Protein Choices   25 g protein   610 kilojoules
                         5 g fat   (145 Calories)

● **Slick Trick:** For one serving, place fish fillet on ovenproof plate, if one is available and cook fish right on the plate. Make sure oven mitts are standing by to handle the hot plate.

Recipe	Food Choices Per Serving	Energy Per Serving		
		kilojoules	Calories	
Roast Beef	3 ⊘ Protein;	690	165	p. 110
Meatballs Ragout	2 ⊘ Protein; 1 ◻ Starchy	730	173	p. 111
Sukiyaki	3 ⊘ Protein; 1 ◗ Fruits & Vegetables	890	213	p. 112
Chicken Sukiyaki	3 ⊘ Protein; 1 ◗ Fruits & Vegetables	890	213	p. 113
Pork Veronique	3 ⊘ Protein; 1 ◗ Fruits & Vegetables	860	205	p. 114
Pork and Ratatouille	3 ⊘ Protein; 1 ◗ Fruits & Vegetables	890	213	p. 115
Liver Creole	3 ⊘ Protein; ½ ◗ Fruits & Vegetables	880	210	p. 116
Herb and Lemon Lamb Chops	2 ⊘ Protein	520	123	p. 117
Chicken in a Package	3 ⊘ Protein	740	177	p. 118
Grandma's Bread Stuffing	1 ◻ Starchy; ½ ▲ Fats & Oils	390	94	p. 119
Lime-Broiled Chicken Breasts	3 ⊘ Protein	710	169	p. 120
Roast Chicken	3 ⊘ Protein	690	165	p. 121
Chicken and Vegetable Stir-Fry	1 ⊘ Protein; 1 ✚ Extra Vegetables; ½ ▲ Fats & Oils	430	102	p. 122
Stir-Braised Scallops with Vegetables	3 ⊘ Protein ½ ◗ Fruits & Vegetables	610	146	p. 123
Foil-Baked Lemon Fish Fillets	3 ⊘ Protein	740	177	p. 124
Foil-Baked Tomato Fish Fillets	3 ⊘ Protein	740	177	p. 125
Crisp Fish Sticks	4 ⊘ Protein; 1 ◻ Starchy	1030	245	p. 126
Dilly Crisp Fish Sticks	4 ⊘ Protein; 1 ◻ Starchy	1030	245	p. 127
Baked Fish Fillets with Walnuts	3 ⊘ Protein	670	159	p. 127
Baked Fish Fillets Parmesan	3 ⊘ Protein	610	145	p. 127

Notes

Make it Meatless

After my first trip to Mexico, I came back with a new recipe for beans. They had appeared in my meals every day while I was away and they were very good.

Now I plan many menus featuring beans and find they make some of the most economical meatless meals. And, as well as being relatively inexpensive as compared to meat meals, they are nutritious and provide dietary fibre.

Legumes, like beans, and lentils provide nutritious but incomplete vegetable protein, not complete animal protein like that found in meat, milk, eggs and cheese. However, when two vegetable proteins, such as beans and rice or legumes and grains, are eaten together, the quality of protein is improved and the combination becomes a complete protein. It is the complete protein that is essential in our diets.

Other combinations that work are rice and lentils, corn and beans, rice and peas, pasta and beans, and brown bread and beans. The nutritional quality of vegetable protein is often improved by a little animal protein and the two then provide complete protein. Macaroni and cheese, or rice pudding containing rice, egg and milk, are examples of this.

The variety of dishes from egg and cheese combinations seems endless — from the simple omelet to the elegant soufflé. You will find recipes for those two in this collection. Both will probably become family favorites.

Pasta and rice dishes also fit into this meatless section. Both are types of starchy carbohydrate and a 125 mL (½ cup) serving can replace a slice of bread as 1 ■ Starchy Choice in a meal.

◀ From top clockwise:
Cheese Zucchini Puff,
Mushroom Lasagna,
Space-Age Barbecued
Beans

Lentil Curry with Cucumbers and Bananas

Preparation time: 5 minutes
Cooking time: 10 to 15 minutes

Curries are often eaten with simply prepared fruits and vegetables to lessen and cool the "heat" of the spice combination. A side dish of cucumbers with yogurt, and sliced bananas, serve that purpose here.

1		medium onion, chopped	1
1		small apple, cored and chopped	1
25	mL	water	2 tbsp
5-10	mL	curry powder	1-2 tsp
2	mL	salt	½ tsp
	Pinch	freshly ground pepper	Pinch
1		can (540 mL/19 oz) lentils	1
250	mL	chopped cucumber	1 cup
50	mL	2% yogurt	¼ cup
½		small banana sliced	½
	Dash	lemon juice	Dash

❶ In a saucepan, combine onion, apple, water, curry to taste, salt and pepper.
❷ Stir-braise over medium-low heat, about 4 minutes or until onion is translucent and apple tender, adding a little more water if pan becomes dry.
❸ Drain and rinse lentils under cold running water; drain well. Stir into apple mixture. Cook, stirring occasionally, about 5 minutes or until heated through.
❹ In a small bowl, combine cucumber and yogurt.
❺ Slice banana; sprinkle with a few drops of lemon juice.
❻ Serve curry with cucumber and banana.

Makes 4 servings

Each serving: 125 mL (½ cup), plus ¼ cucumber and ¼ banana slice

½ ◨ Protein Choice	24 g carbohydrate	520 kilojoules
1 ◻ Starchy Choice	7 g protein	(124 Calories)
1 ◪ Fruits & Vegetables Choice		

Pasta E Fagioli — Pasta and Beans

Preparation time: 20 minutes
Cooking time: 10 minutes

When pasta and beans are eaten together, they complement each other and provide complete protein to the diet. On their own, each one is short of one or more of the essential amino acids of a complete protein and therefore supplies incomplete protein. You'll find this meal-in-a-pot is not only nutritious, it is economical too because both legumes (beans) and pasta are reasonably priced.

250 mL	macaroni or other small shell pasta	1	cup
1	can (398 mL/14 oz) kidney beans	1	
1	can (398 mL/14 oz) tomatoes	1	
250 mL	diced carrots	1	cup
2	stalks celery, diagonally sliced	2	
1	medium onion, chopped	1	
1	clove garlic, finely chopped	1	
2 mL	dried thyme	½	tsp
2 mL	dried fines herbes*	½	tsp
2 mL	salt	½	tsp
Pinch	freshly ground black pepper	Pinch	

❶ In a large saucepan, in 1.5 L (6 cups) lightly salted boiling water, cook macaroni about 10 minutes or until *al dente* (tender but firm); place in strainer or sieve to drain. Pour beans over macaroni. Rinse well under cold running water; drain well.

❷ In same saucepan, combine tomatoes, carrots, celery, onion, garlic, thyme, fines herbes, salt and pepper. Bring to a boil and cook for 3 minutes.

❸ Stir macaroni and beans into tomato mixture. Reduce heat; cover and simmer for 7 to 10 minutes or until vegetables are tender. Add a little water if liquid evaporates too quickly.

Makes 4 servings

Each serving: 250 mL (1 cup)

1 ⊘ Protein Choice
2 ☐ Starchy Choices

33 g carbohydrate   730 kilojoules
 8 g protein   (173 Calories)
 1 g fat

● **Timely Tip:** *Fines Herbes, a mixture of oregano, basil and parsley can be found in supermarket herb racks.

Twice-Cooked Beans

Preparation time: 5 minutes
Cooking time: 10 minutes

Mexicans fry cooked beans with flavorings until they are pulpy but still moist. They call them "Frijoles" which means refried beans. Mashed potatoes, move over! Refried beans are taking your place at many tables.

1	can (540 mL/19 oz) pinto, Romano or kidney beans	1
5 mL	corn oil	1 tbsp
125 mL	chopped onion	½ cup
Pinch	ground coriander	Pinch
Pinch	chili powder	Pinch

❶ Drain beans, reserving liquid.
❷ In a saucepan or skillet, heat oil; add beans, onion, coriander and chili powder. Stir and mash with the back of a large spoon or potato masher until beans are partially mashed. Simmer, stirring frequently, for 5 to 10 minutes or until beans are the desired consistency, adding a small amount of reserved bean liquid if needed.

Makes 3 servings

Each serving: 125 mL (½ cup)
1 ⊘ Protein Choice
2 ☐ Starchy Choices

29 g carbohydrate   790 kilojoules
11 g protein   (187 Calories)
 3 g fat

Mexican Beans and Rice

Preparation time: 20 minutes
Cooking time: 15 minutes

When dried beans (legumes) and rice are combined and eaten together in a dish like this, they complement each other and provide complete protein that is equivalent to meat. Neither beans nor rice supply complete protein. If you prefer more "heat" in the flavor of this Mexican-style hotpot, add a bit more chili powder and a few drops of hot pepper sauce.

1	medium onion, chopped	1
1	green pepper, seeded and chopped	1
1	can (540 mL/19 oz) tomatoes	1
2 mL	chili powder	½ tsp
2 mL	Worcestershire sauce	½ tsp
1 mL	celery seed	¼ tsp
1	can (540 mL/19 oz) kidney, Romano or pinto beans, drained and rinsed	1
250 mL	cooked brown or white long grain rice	1 cup
Pinch	freshly ground pepper	Pinch
75 mL	shredded Cheddar cheese	⅓ cup

❶ In a 2 L (8 cup) saucepan, combine onion, green pepper, tomatoes, chili powder, Worcestershire sauce and celery seed. Bring to a boil over medium heat; reduce heat and simmer for 5 minutes, stirring once or twice.
❷ Add rinsed beans, rice and pepper. Stir gently to combine. Continue to simmer 10 minutes longer for flavors to blend.
❸ Serve sprinkled with shredded cheese.

Makes 6 servings

Each serving: 200 mL (¾ cup)

1 ▨ Protein Choice
1 ◻ Starchy Choice
1 ▨ Fruits & Vegetables Choice

26 g carbohydrate
8 g protein
3 g fat

680 kilojoules
(163 Calories)

Quickest Ever Chili

Preparation time: 10 minutes
Cooking time: 15 minutes

If you only have an hour to make your meal, eat it and clean up afterward, then this is for you. All the ingredients simmer together for a few minutes, and a bowl of hot chili is ready. Tofu, soybean curd, adds protein to the mixture.

2	stalks celery, thinly sliced	2
1	medium onion, chopped	1
1	green pepper, chopped	1
125 mL	chicken broth	½ cup
1	can (213 mL/7½ oz) tomato sauce	1
10-15 mL	chili powder	2-3 tsp
1	can (540 mL/19 oz) Romano or pinto beans, drained and rinsed	1
1	block tofu (6 x 6 x 4 cm/2½ x 2½ x 1½ in), 140 g	1
Pinch	freshly ground pepper	Pinch

❶ In a saucepan, combine celery, onion, green pepper, chicken broth, tomato sauce and chili powder.
❷ Cook over medium heat, stirring occasionally, for 5 minutes.
❸ Stir in beans.
❹ Press tofu between paper towels to remove some of the moisture. Cut into small cubes; stir into bean mixture. Simmer about 10 minutes.
❺ Serve in bowls or deep plates.

Makes 4 servings, 750 mL (3 cups)

Each serving: 200 mL (¾ cup)
1 ▨ Protein Choice
2 ▨ Starchy Choices

28 g carbohydrate   810 kilojoules
11 g protein   (192 Calories)
 4 g fat

Italian Beans and Tomatoes

Preparation time: 5 minutes
Cooking time: 15 minutes

*For a rich tomatoey sauce like this one, I use Italian plum toma-
toes because they are pulpier than regular tomatoes. However,
regular canned tomatoes can be used if the plum are not
available.*

1	medium onion, finely chopped	1
2	cloves garlic, mashed and chopped	2
5 mL	dried sage	1 tsp
1	can (540 mL/19 oz) Italian plum tomatoes	1
1	can (540 mL/19 oz) Romano beans	1
5 mL	bulk granulated artificial sweetener, like SugarTwin, equivalent to 5 mL (1 tsp) sugar	1 tsp
2 mL	lemon juice	½ tsp

❶ In a saucepan, combine onion, garlic, sage and tomatoes.
❷ Cook over medium heat, stirring and mashing the tomatoes
with the back of a spoon, for about 5 minutes or until onion is
tender.
❸ Drain and rinse beans; stir into tomato mixture.
❹ Cook about 10 minutes longer or until half the liquid
evaporates.
❺ Stir in sweetener and lemon juice and serve.

Makes 4 servings

Each serving: 200 mL (¾ cup)
2 ⬛ Starchy Choices   28 g carbohydrate   580 kilojoules
                                    4 g protein   (137 Calories)
                                    1 g fat

Variation:

Italian Beans, Tomatoes and Mushrooms: Chop 8 medium
mushrooms and add to the tomato mixture with the beans.

Calculations as above

Space-Age Barbecued Beans

Preparation time: 10 minutes
Cooking time: 20 to 25 minutes

When it is your turn to have the gang over after a football game or track meet, have a pot of these beans ready to reheat. With the beans, I like to serve Keeps-A-Week Coleslaw, (recipe, p. 80), which can also be made ahead.

125 mL	tubetti or macaroni	½ cup
1	can (540 mL/19 oz) red kidney beans	1
1	can (540 mL/19 oz) white kidney beans	1
125 mL	chicken broth	½ cup
2	medium (15 cm/6 in) zucchini, chopped	2
1	medium onion, chopped	1
1	can (213 mL/7½ oz) tomato sauce	1
15 mL	bulk granulated artificial sweetener, like SugarTwin, equivalent to 15 mL (1 tbsp) sugar	1 tbsp
10 mL	Dijon mustard	2 tsp
10 mL	vinegar	2 tsp
5 mL	horseradish	1 tsp

❶ In a saucepan of rapidly boiling water, cook tubetti about 12 minutes or until *al dente* (tender but firm).
❷ Pour tubetti into a sieve or colander to drain; add both red and white beans to drain, then rinse.
❸ In another saucepan, combine broth, zucchini, onion, tomato sauce, sweetener, mustard, vinegar and horseradish. Bring to a boil; reduce heat and simmer for 5 minutes.
❹ Stir in tubetti and beans. Continue to cook, stirring occasionally, for 15 minutes. Or, transfer mixture to a baking dish or casserole and bake in a 180°C (350°F) oven for 15 to 20 minutes or until warmed through.

Makes 8 servings

Each serving: 200 mL (¾ cup)
½ ▨ Protein Choice
2 ◻ Starchy Choices

28 g carbohydrate   680 kilojoules
 8 g protein   (162 Calories)
 2 g fat

Spanish Rice with Chick Peas

Preparation time: 10 minutes
Cooking time: 15 minutes

Rice and the legume, chick peas, complement each other to make this a combination that supplies complete protein. It rates with individuals practising a vegetarian routine.

2	stalks celery, chopped	2
1	medium onion, chopped	1
1	green pepper, chopped	1
1	clove garlic, chopped	1
1	can (540 mL/19 oz) tomatoes	1
2 mL	Worcestershire sauce	½ tsp
3	whole cloves	3
1	can (540 mL/19 oz) chick peas, drained and rinsed	1
250 mL	cooked long grain rice	1 cup
Pinch	freshly ground pepper	Pinch
50 g	shredded mozzarella cheese (125 mL/½ cup)	2 oz

❶ In a 2 L (8 cup) saucepan, combine celery, onion, green pepper, garlic, tomatoes, Worcestershire sauce and cloves.
❷ Bring to a boil over medium heat; reduce heat and simmer, stirring once or twice, for 5 minutes.
❸ Stir in rinsed chick peas, rice and pepper. Continue to cook, stirring occasionally, for 10 minutes or until warmed through.
❹ Serve sprinkled with shredded cheese.

Makes 6 servings

Each serving: 200 mL (¾ cup)
1 🟦 Protein Choice
1 ⬜ Starchy Choice
1 🟦 Fruits & Vegetables Choice

25 g carbohydrate   670 kilojoules
8 g protein   (159 Calories)
3 g fat

Mushroom Lasagna

Preparation time: 30 minutes
Cooking time: 1 hour

You can hardly tell there is no meat in this lasagna. It is a novel departure from the usual and is bound to be popular even for company dinners. A bonus — single portions can be frozen to be reheated later.

15	mL	olive oil	1 tbsp
1		medium onion, chopped	1
1		clove garlic, minced	1
500	g	mushrooms, chopped	1 lb
2		stalks celery, chopped	2
½		sweet red or green pepper, chopped	½
1		can (398 mL/14 oz) Italian tomatoes	1
2	mL	each dried thyme, oregano and basil	½ tsp
	Pinch	freshly ground pepper	Pinch
4		lasagna noodles	4
250	g	2% cottage cheese	½ lb
250	mL	shredded skim milk mozzarella cheese (100 g/4 oz)	1 cup
25	mL	freshly grated Parmesan cheese	2 tbsp

❶ In a 2 L (8 cup) saucepan, combine oil, onion and garlic. Stir-cook over medium heat about 3 minutes or until onion is limp. Stir in mushrooms, celery and sweet pepper. Continue to cook over medium-high heat, stirring, until liquid evaporates (this happens quickly).

❷ Add tomatoes, thyme, oregano, basil and pepper. Bring to a boil; reduce heat and simmer, stirring occasionally, for 15 to 20 minutes or until thickened and saucy.

❸ In a large saucepan, cook lasagna noodles in 3 L (12 cups) rapidly boiling, lightly salted water, about 8 minutes or until *al dente* (tender but firm).

❹ To assemble lasagna, spread 125 mL (½ cup) of the sauce on bottom of a 20 cm (8 in) baking dish. Top with single layer of lasagna noodles cut to fit dish, using ends to fill spaces.

Spread with half the cottage cheese and half the mozzarella, 250 mL (1 cup) sauce and another layer of noodles. Spread with remaining cottage cheese and sauce. Sprinkle with remaining mozzarella and Parmesan.

❺ Bake in a 180°C (350°F) oven for 30 minutes or until heated through.

Makes 4 servings

Each serving: ¼ baking dish of lasagna

3 ▨ Protein Choices	25 g carbohydrate	1210 kilojoules
1 ▢ Starchy Choice	27 g protein	(289 Calories)
1 ▨ Fruits & Vegetables Choice	9 g fat	

● **Timely Tip:** To freeze lasagna, first cool the baked lasagna and cut it into squares. Wrap each portion in foil, making sure you label the package with name, date and serving size, then freeze. Keep in the freezer up to 3 months. Reheat in a 160°C (325°F) oven in the foil for 15 minutes or unwrap, place on plate and reheat in the microwave oven.

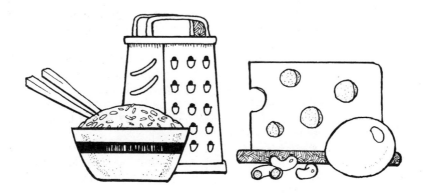

Cheese Zucchini Puff

Preparation time: 10 minutes
Cooking time: 50 minutes

Produce departments always seem to have zucchini available and gardens overflow with them when they are in season. And creative cooks are always coming up with new recipes for the vegetable. This innovative, soufflé-like dish is one of them and it rates a 10 as a meatless lunch or supper dish.

500 mL	shredded zucchini (2 medium, each 15 cm/6 in)	2 cups
1	medium onion, chopped	1
125 mL	dry bread crumbs	½ cup
125 mL	shredded Cheddar cheese	½ cup
15 mL	finely chopped fresh basil OR 5 mL (1 tsp) dried	1 tbsp
1	egg	1
125 mL	skim milk	½ cup
2 mL	salt	1 tsp
Pinch	freshly ground pepper	Pinch

❶ In a bowl, combine zucchini, onion, bread crumbs, cheese and basil.
❷ In a separate bowl, combine egg, milk, salt and pepper; beat lightly.
❸ Pour egg mixture into zucchini mixture; stir well. Spoon into a 1.5 L (6 cup) casserole or baking dish.
❹ Bake in a 180°C (350°F) oven for 50 minutes or until top is lightly browned and tester, inserted halfway between outside and centre of dish, comes out clean.

Makes 4 servings

Each serving: 200 mL (¾ cup)

1 🅿 Protein Choice   15 g carbohydrate   590 kilojoules
1 ◻ Starchy Choice   9 g protein   (141 Calories)
                                       5 g fat

Crustless Spinach Quiche

Preparation time: 15 minutes
Cooking time: 45 minutes

Boys and men like this spinach, cheese and egg "pie" and don't even miss the crust. A wedge or two makes a meal. A bunch of crunchy pieces of **++** *Extra Vegetables is all that is needed as an accompaniment.*

5 mL	butter or margarine	1	tsp
1	pkg (300 g) frozen chopped spinach, drained	1	
50 mL	chopped onion	¼	cup
250 mL	2% cottage cheese	1	cup
175 mL	shredded Edam cheese (125 g/5 oz)	⅔	cup
125 mL	freshly grated Parmesan cheese	½	cup
125 mL	skim milk	½	cup
2	eggs	2	
75 mL	whole wheat flour	⅓	cup
5 mL	baking powder	1	tsp
5 mL	dried sweet basil	1	tsp
1 mL	ground nutmeg	¼	tsp
2 mL	salt	½	tsp
Pinch	freshly ground pepper	Pinch	

❶ Grease a 23 cm (9 in) pie plate with butter.
❷ In a bowl, combine spinach, onion, cottage cheese, Edam and Parmesan cheeses.
❸ In a blender or food processor, combine milk, eggs, flour, baking powder, basil, nutmeg, salt and pepper. Process at high speed for 1 minute. (Alternatively, in a bowl, whisk ingredients together vigorously.)
❹ Pour egg mixture over vegetable mixture; mix well. Pour into prepared pie plate.
❺ Bake in a 180°C (350°F) oven for 45 minutes or until knife inserted near centre comes out clean. Let stand for 5 minutes before serving.

Makes 8 servings

Each serving: ⅛ of spinach pie
2 ⬛ Protein Choices
½ ⬛ Starchy Choice

7 g carbohydrate   620 kilojoules
14 g protein   (147 Calories)
7 g fat

French Omelet

Preparation time: 2 minutes
Cooking time: 8 minutes

*Lightly stirring the eggs while they cook develops a fluffy,
evenly cooked omelet, perfect for holding your favorite fillings.*

4	medium eggs	4
15 mL	water	1 tbsp
1 mL	salt	¼ tsp
5 mL	unsalted butter	1 tsp
	Parsley, celery or tomato half	

❶ Crack eggs into bowl; add water and salt. Beat lightly with a
fork or whisk just until egg is well mixed, but do not overbeat.
❷ In a 15 cm (6 in) nonstick omelet pan, melt half the butter
over medium heat. With a brush, coat bottom and sides of pan.
❸ Pour half the egg mixture into the hot pan; shake the pan as
omelet cooks and immediately stir the eggs with a fork, holding
the tines of the fork parallel with the bottom of the pan and al-
lowing the liquid or uncooked portion to run under the cooked
portion.
❹ When eggs seem to coagulate, spread them over bottom of
pan in an even layer.
❺ For an unfilled omelet, tip pan slightly and fold the half
nearer the handle over the opposite half.
❻ For a filled omelet, put filling in a line along the side opposite
the pan handle.
❼ Using handle, tip pan toward the filled side; slide a lifter
under the unfilled half, lift it and fold it over the filled half.
❽ Push omelet to centre of pan and continue cooking about
1 minute longer to set the omelet and allow the underside to
turn slightly golden brown.
❾ Hold a warmed plate in the left hand; grip omelet pan so that
your thumb is on top of the handle. Tilt the pan and plate toward
each other. Tip pan completely over plate so omelet slides out
onto plate. (Place in a very low oven to keep warm.)
❿ Make second omelet with remaining butter and eggs.
⓫ Garnish with sprig of parsley, celery or tomato slice.

Makes 2 servings

Each serving: 1 omelet (2 eggs)

2 ✪ Protein Choices	12 g protein	660 kilojoules
1 ▲ Fats & Oils Choice	12 g fat	(156 Calories)

Variations:

Cheese Omelet:
1 Sprinkle 25 mL (2 tbsp) shredded mozzarella or Edam cheese on half of each cooked 2-egg omelet before folding omelet.

Each serving: 1 omelet (2 eggs)

2 ▨ Protein Choices
2 ▲ Fats & Oils Choices

1 g carbohydrate
15 g protein
17 g fat

910 kilojoules
(217 Calories)

Mushroom Omelet:
1 In a saucepan combine 125 mL (½ cup) chicken or beef broth, 15 mL (1 tbsp) chopped onion and 6 sliced mushrooms.
2 Bring to a boil, reduce heat and simmer, stirring, about 3 or 4 minutes or until liquid evaporates.
3 Sprinkle with 2 mL (½ tsp) lemon juice and freshly ground pepper.
4 Spread half of mushroom mixture on each 2-egg omelet before folding omelet.

Each serving: 1 omelet (2 eggs)

2 ▨ Protein Choices
1 ▲ Fats & Oils Choice

12 g protein
12 g fat

660 kilojoules
(156 Calories)

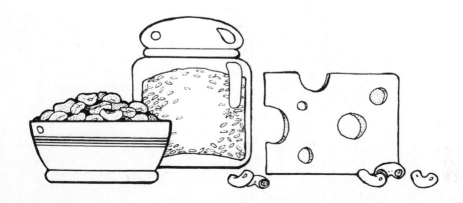

Recipe	Food Choices Per Serving	Energy Per Serving kilojoules Calories	
Lentil Curry with Cucumbers and Bananas	½ ⊘ Protein; 1 ☐ Starchy; 1 ◢ Fruits & Vegetables	520	124	p. 132
Pasta E Fagioli (Pasta and Beans)	1 ⊘ Protein; 2 ☐ Starchy	730	173	p. 133
Twice-Cooked Beans	1 ⊘ Protein; 2 ☐ Starchy	790	187	p. 134
Mexican Beans and Rice	1 ⊘ Protein; 1 ☐ Starchy; 1 ◢ Fruits & Vegetables	680	163	p. 135
Quickest Ever Chili	1 ⊘ Protein; 2 ☐ Starchy	810	192	p. 136
Italian Beans & Tomatoes	2 ☐ Starchy	580	137	p. 137
Italian Beans, Tomatoes and Mushrooms	2 ☐ Starchy	580	137	p. 137
Space-Age Barbecued Beans	½ ⊘ Protein; 2 ☐ Starchy	680	162	p. 138
Spanish Rice with Chick Peas	1 ⊘ Protein; 1 ☐ Starchy; 1 ◢ Fruits & Vegetables	670	159	p. 139
Mushroom Lasagna	3 ⊘ Protein; 1 ☐ Starchy; 1 ◢ Fruits & Vegetables	1210	289	p. 140
Cheese Zucchini Puff	1 ⊘ Protein; 1 ☐ Starchy	590	141	p. 142
Crustless Spinach Quiche	2 ⊘ Protein; ½ ☐ Starchy	620	147	p. 143
French Omelet	2 ⊘ Protein; 1 ▲ Fats & Oils	660	156	p. 144
Cheese Omelet	2 ⊘ Protein; 2 ▲ Fats & Oils	910	217	p. 145
Mushroom Omelet	2 ⊘ Protein; 1 ▲ Fats & Oils	660	156	p. 145

Notes

Vegetable Variations

It puzzles me when I realize some people think vegetables are blah and boring.

Every time I visit a farmer's market or walk down the fresh produce aisle of the supermarket I feel excited. What an array! Every color of the rainbow is there before my eyes along with every shape imaginable. Red round tomatoes, orange pointed carrots, green leafy lettuce, purple plump eggplant, yellow stringy beans. And there is just as fabulous a selection along the aisles of the canned goods and frozen packages.

Vegetables do add assorted colors, flavors, shapes and textures. A dinner without them would be boring and unbalanced. And it is the vegetables in our diet that supply us with carbohydrates, important vitamins and minerals plus dietary fibre. The only vegetables I find blah are the ones that are overcooked. They are dull and lifeless.

My rule with vegetables is to cook them only until tender-crisp. They are best that way, and more tasty than when they are flabby and mushy.

If you choose canned vegetables for your meals, remember they just have to be warmed; processing has already cooked them. Following the recipes here you can select a few new and tasty vegetable dishes, everything from a colorful mixture to a blend of two together.

Note: Some vegetables are high in dietary fibre and low in available carbohydrate. They may be counted as ✚✚ Extra Vegetables if they are eaten in the portion size indicated with the recipe, because only part of the carbohydrate is considered available to the blood sugar.

◄ **From top clockwise:**
Braised Vegetable
Medley, Parmesan
Tomatoes, Schnippled
Green Beans

Baked Asparagus

Preparation time: 10 minutes
Cooking time: 15 minutes

Asparagus really does have the color and taste of Spring if you steam it in just the water clinging to it after being rinsed.

20	stalks asparagus	20
Pinch	freshly ground pepper	Pinch
½	lemon, cut into 4 wedges	½

❶ Rinse asparagus stalks, place them in a single or double layer in a (20 cm/8 in) baking dish or covered casserole.
❷ Sprinkle with pepper and the juice from 1 lemon wedge.
❸ Cover dish tightly with foil or its own cover. Bake in a 180°C (350°F) oven for 15 minutes or until tender-crisp.
❹ Serve 1 wedge lemon with each 5 stalks of asparagus.

Makes 4 servings

Each serving: 5 asparagus stalks

1 ➕➕ Extra Vegetables

3 g carbohydrate   70 kilojoules
1 g protein   (16 Calories)

See Note, p. 149

Braised Vegetable Medley

Preparation time: 7 minutes
Cooking time: 15 minutes

A medley of vegetables adds excitement to a meal. When an assortment of vegetables cooks together in the braising liquid the flavors mingle.

250 mL	chopped onion (½ Spanish onion)	1 cup
250 mL	cubed zucchini, 1 medium (15 cm/6 in)	1 cup
250 mL	cubed butternut squash	1 cup
250 mL	cubed carrot (3 medium)	1 cup
250 mL	sliced celery (3 stalks)	1 cup
125 mL	chicken broth	½ cup
Pinch	freshly ground pepper	Pinch

❶ In a 2 L (8 cup) saucepan, combine onion, zucchini, squash, carrot, celery, chicken broth and pepper. Bring to a boil over medium heat; reduce heat, cover and simmer over medium-low heat about 12 minutes or until carrots and celery are tender-crisp, and zucchini and squash are tender.

❷ Remove cover and if there is liquid in bottom of pan, continue to cook, stirring occasionally, for 1 to 2 minutes to allow most of liquid to evaporate.

Makes 6 servings

Each serving: 125 mL (½ cup)

½ ▱ Fruits & Vegetables Choice   6 g carbohydrate   120 kilojoules
                                    1 g protein   (28 Calories)

Ginger Orange Carrots

Preparation time: 5 minutes
Cooking time: 15 to 20 minutes

My family loves these spicy and sweet carrots and so will yours.

300 g	carrots, thinly sliced (500 mL/2 cups)	10 oz
1	small orange	1
1 mL	ground ginger	¼ tsp
5 mL	unsalted butter	1 tsp

❶ Scrub carrots. Peel if outside peel is coarse. Cut into very thin slices to make about 500 mL (2 cups).

❷ Grate orange rind to measure 5 mL (1 tsp). Squeeze juice from orange; reserve.

❸ In saucepan, combine carrot slices, orange rind, half the orange juice, ginger and butter. Braise, covered, over medium heat for 12 minutes.

❹ Add remaining orange juice; cook, uncovered, just until carrots are tender and juice has evaporated.

Makes 4 servings

Each serving: 125 mL (½ cup)

1 ▰ Fruits & Vegetables Choice   11 g carbohydrate   240 kilojoules
                                    1 g protein   (57 Calories)
                                    1 g fat

Schnippled Green Beans

Preparation time: 10 minutes

This snappy salad is similar to one made by Mennonite cooks in the Kitchener-Waterloo area of Ontario. Serve it either as a vegetable or a salad.

1	pkg (300 g) cut or frenched frozen green beans (375 mL/1½ cups)	1
2	green onions, sliced	2
25 mL	2% yogurt	2 tbsp
10 mL	vinegar	2 tsp
	Artificial sweetener, like SugarTwin, equivalent to 5 mL (1 tsp) sugar	
Pinch	freshly ground pepper	Pinch

❶ Defrost beans ahead (or place frozen beans in a sieve and pour boiling water over, then cool under cold running water; drain well).
❷ In a bowl, combine beans and green onions.
❸ In a small dish, combine yogurt, vinegar and sweetener; mix well.
❹ Pour yogurt sauce over beans. Toss to coat. Season with pepper and serve.

Makes 3 servings

Each serving: 125 mL (½ cup)

1 **++** Extra Vegetables   4 g carbohydrate   80 kilojoules
                                    1 g protein   (20 Calories)

See Note, p. 149

Braised Red Cabbage

Preparation time: 10 minutes
Cooking time: 15 minutes

Cabbage is at its best when it is quickly cooked before any strong flavors develop. If you have a processor, use it to shred the cabbage. If not, the shredding is done easily with a sharp knife. A dull one bruises the cabbage.

½	medium red cabbage, finely shredded 1 L (4 cups)	½
1	small onion, chopped	1
3	whole allspice berries	3
2	whole cloves	2
5 mL	grated orange rind	1 tsp
125 mL	water	½ cup
50 mL	orange juice	¼ cup
10 mL	soy sauce	2 tsp
10 mL	vinegar	2 tsp
5 mL	cornstarch	1 tsp

❶ Finely shred cabbage.
❷ In a large skillet or 2 L (8 cup) saucepan, combine cabbage, onion, allspice, cloves, orange rind, and water.
❸ Bring to a boil, reduce heat and stir-braise (braise while stirring occasionally) for 12 minutes or until cabbage is tender-crisp. Add a little extra water, if required, to prevent cabbage from sticking to the bottom of the pan.
❹ In a small dish, combine orange juice, soy sauce and vinegar. Stir in cornstarch until smooth.
❺ Stir into cabbage mixture, continuing to cook and stirring until a thin sauce coats cabbage.

Makes 4 servings

Each serving: about 200 mL (¾ cup)
½ ◼ Fruits & Vegetables Choice   6 g carbohydrate   100 kilojoules
                                                             (24 Calories)

Steamed Leeks and Zucchini

Preparation time: 5 minutes
Cooking time: 5 minutes

Leeks look like very large green onions. They are milder than regular onions and when they are available, they are a treat. Here they are simply steamed with zucchini and spice for a little added pizzazz.

3	medium leeks	3
3	medium zucchini (each 15 cm/6 in)	3
Pinch	each ground cumin and nutmeg	Pinch
50 mL	chopped sweet red pepper OR seeded chopped tomato (optional)	¼ cup

❶ Trim coarse green leaves from leeks; rinse under cold running water. Cut into 1 cm (½ in) slices.
❷ Rinse zucchini. Remove stem and flower ends. Cut into 1 cm (½ in) slices.
❸ In a steamer basket or perforated pan, combine leeks and zucchini; sprinkle with cumin and nutmeg. Place over saucepan of boiling water. Cover and steam for 4 to 5 minutes or until leeks are transparent and zucchini is tender crisp. Add chopped pepper, if desired. Toss gently and serve.

Makes 4 servings

Each serving: 125 mL (½ cup)
1 **++** Extra Vegetables

4 g carbohydrate   80 kilojoules
1 g protein   (20 Calories)

See Note, p. 149

Turnip Cubes

Preparation time: 5 minutes
Cooking time: 12 minutes

Both the purple-tipped, small white turnip and the yellow rutabaga are known as turnips. Either one cooks up quickly when it is cut into small cubes, and the resulting flavor is mellow.

500 g	white turnips or rutabaga	1 lb
Pinch	mace or powdered cumin	Pinch
Pinch	freshly ground pepper	Pinch

❶ Peel turnips and cut into small 1 cm (½ in) cubes.
❷ In a saucepan, combine turnips with enough water to cover. Bring to a boil, cover and cook about 12 minutes or until fork-tender.
❸ Drain and sprinkle with mace and pepper. Toss gently and serve.

Makes 4 servings

Each serving: 125 mL (½ cup)
½ 🥕 Fruits & Vegetables Choice   5 g carbohydrate   80 kilojoules
                                                              (20 Calories)

Parmesan Tomatoes

Preparation time: 5 minutes
Cooking time: 7 minutes

Hot, juicy, baked tomatoes that hold their shape are as pretty as a picture served beside a barbecued or baked steak, chop or chicken breast.

2	medium tomatoes	2
10 mL	freshly grated Parmesan cheese	2 tsp
2 mL	dried basil	½ tsp
Pinch	freshly ground pepper	Pinch

❶ Cut tomatoes in half. Place in a small baking dish cut side up.
❷ Combine cheese, basil and pepper. Sprinkle over tomatoes.
❸ Bake in a 160°C (325°F) oven for about 7 minutes or until heated through.

Makes 4 servings

Each serving: 1 tomato half
1 ➕ Extra Vegetables   2 g carbohydrate   50 kilojoules
                                   1 g protein   (12 Calories)

See Note, p. 149

Cheesy Chive Potatoes

Preparation time: 20 minutes

Cooked potatoes are more exciting when dressed up a bit with cottage cheese and chives. Roughly mashed means there are still small chunks of potato in the mixture. For this dish, a lumpy texture is more interesting than one that is mashed smooth.

3	medium potatoes, boiled or baked* and peeled	3
125 mL	2% cottage cheese	½ cup
15 mL	fresh or frozen chopped chives	1 tbsp
1 mL	salt	¼ tsp
Pinch	freshly ground pepper	Pinch

❶ If potatoes have been refrigerated, place them in a steamer over boiling water for about 10 minutes.
❷ In a warm ovenproof bowl, roughly mash potatoes; stir in cottage cheese, chives, salt and pepper.
❸ Serve immediately or keep warm in 100°C (200°F) oven.

Makes 6 servings

Each serving: 125 mL (½ cup)
1 ◻ Starchy Choice   12 g carbohydrate   270 kilojoules
                              4 g protein   (64 Calories)

To Microwave: In a glass bowl, roughly mash potatoes; stir in cottage cheese, chives, salt and pepper. Cover lightly with plastic wrap. Heat in microwave oven on High about 5 minutes, rotating bowl ½-turn halfway through the heating time.

● **Timely Tip:** *For baked potatoes, see Roasted Potato Skins (recipe, p. 45)

Baked Potato Chips

Preparation time: 10 minutes
Cooking time: 20 to 30 minutes

Potato lovers and others will adore these. It's amazing how far just a little butter will go when a small brush is used for spreading it on the potato slices. Yes, there is enough to give all the potato slices a light glaze of buttery flavor.

2	baking potatoes	2
15 mL	melted butter	2 tsp
	Salt and freshly ground pepper	

❶ Scrub potatoes well, but do not peel.
❷ Place one oven rack in upper third of oven, the second one in the lower third of oven. Preheat oven to 250°C (500°F).
❸ Lightly brush about 5 mL (1 tsp) melted butter on 2 nonstick baking sheets.
❹ Cut potatoes crosswise into 3 mm (⅛ in) thick slices, 12 per half potato. Rinse with cold water, drain, and pat dry with paper towels.
❺ Arrange in single layer on prepared baking sheets. Brush remaining butter very lightly across top of each potato slice.
❻ Place one baking sheet on each rack. Bake for 10 minutes. Switch pan positions and bake about 10 minutes longer or until potatoes are crisp and browned around edges.
❼ Transfer to serving platter. Sprinkle with a little bit of salt and pepper. Serve immediately.

Makes 4 servings

Each serving: ½ potato (12 chips)
1 ☐ Starchy Choice
½ ▲ Fats and Oils Choice

12 g carbohydrate   350 kilojoules
2 g protein   (83 Calories)
3 g fat

Squash and Potato Purée

Preparation time: 7 minutes
Cooking time: 10 minutes

I often vary the flavor of vegetables by puréeing or mashing two or three of them together as in this squash and potato combo. It is just another way to show that vegetables never should be boring.

½	butternut or acorn squash, 250 g (½ lb)	½
1	medium potato	1
1	whole clove	1
1 mL	ground cumin	¼ tsp

❶ Peel squash and potato; dice or slice.
❷ In a saucepan, combine vegetables with clove and enough water to cover. Bring to a boil; reduce heat, cover and cook for 7 to 10 minutes or until soft.
❸ Drain; remove and discard clove.
❹ Mash by hand with cumin, or place in food processor equipped with steel blade; add cumin and process until puréed. Serve.

Makes 4 servings

Each serving: 125 mL (½ cup)
1 ▰ Fruits & Vegetables Choice   11 g carbohydrate   220 kilojoules
                                         2 g protein   (52 Calories)

Braised Sweet Peppers

Preparation time: 5 minutes
Cooking time: 7 minutes

Bright slivers of red and green peppers will definitely add sparkle to meals that might otherwise seem a little dull.

1	large sweet green pepper	1
1	large sweet red pepper	1
1	small onion, chopped	1
125 mL	chicken broth	½ cup
5 mL	grated fresh ginger OR 1 mL (¼ tsp) dried	1 tsp
Pinch	freshly ground pepper	Pinch

❶ Cut peppers in half and remove seeds. Cut into long thin strips.
❷ In a skillet or saucepan, combine pepper strips, onion and chicken broth.
❸ Bring to a boil, reduce heat, and stir-braise (braise while stirring occasionally) for 5 to 7 minutes or until peppers are just tender-crisp. Add a little extra water, if required, to prevent peppers from sticking to the bottom of the pan.
❹ Sprinkle with ginger and pepper. Toss gently and serve.

Makes 4 servings

Each serving: ½ large pepper in strips
1 **++** Extra Vegetables

3 g carbohydrate
1 g protein

50 kilojoules
(12 Calories)

See Note, p. 149

Recipe	Food Choices Per Serving	Energy Per Serving		
		kilojoules	Calories	
Baked Asparagus	1 ++ Extra Vegetables	70	16	p. 150
Braised Vegetable Medley	½ ◢ Fruits & Vegetables	120	28	p. 150
Ginger Orange Carrots	1 ◢ Fruits & Vegetables	240	57	p. 151
Schnippled Green Beans	1 ++ Extra Vegetables	80	20	p. 152
Braised Red Cabbage	½ ◢ Fruits & Vegetables	100	24	p. 153
Steamed Leeks and Zucchini	1 ++ Extra Vegetables	80	20	p. 154
Turnip Cubes	½ ◢ Fruits & Vegetables	80	20	p. 154
Parmesan Tomatoes	1 ++ Extra Vegetables	50	12	p. 155
Cheesy Chive Potatoes	1 ☐ Starchy	270	64	p. 156
Baked Potato Chips	1 ☐ Starchy; ½ ▲ Fats & Oils	350	83	p. 157
Squash and Potato Purée	1 ◢ Fruits & Vegetables	220	52	p. 158
Braised Sweet Peppers	1 ++ Extra Vegetables	50	12	p. 159

Notes

Bake it Fresh

Every kitchen should turn into a bakery now and then and every cook should be a baker because baking really is fun. Baked goods please everyone, seniors and kids alike.

Kneading real bread made with yeast is pleasant and relaxing. It is also fascinating as you feel the dough become elastic under your hands. Watching quick breads, such as muffins and scones, plump up as they bake and brown is also exciting.

Smelling the sensational sweet, spicy and buttery aromas of cookies baking might create a problem because you will probably want to sneak one or two as soon as they come out of the oven.

Sharing the home-baked goodness of crusty, grainy rolls, moist fruity muffins, or crunchy chocolaty cookies is just as much fun. You will love it when they rave about your baking.

◀ From top clockwise:
Orange Cornmeal
Muffins, Apple Spice
Squares, Snacking
Cake, Double Chocolate
Oatmeal Cookies

Auntie Kay's Magic Bread

A good yeast dough can be made into all sorts of bread. This one is one of the simplest but still the best I have ever made and that is why it is the only one in the book. My daughter, Susan, calls it magic because from it we make bread, hamburger buns, pita, English muffins and even pizza crust as you will see in the following instructions.

5 mL	granulated sugar	1 tsp
50 mL	warm water	¼ cup
1	pkg active dry yeast OR 15 mL (1 tbsp)	1
250 mL	water	1 cup
500 mL	all-purpose flour	2 cups
250 mL	whole wheat flour	1 cup
5 mL	salt	1 tsp
5 mL	corn oil	1 tsp
25 mL	corn meal	2 tbsp

❶ In a small bowl or measure, combine sugar and 50 mL (¼ cup) warm water. Sprinkle yeast over top and let stand for 10 minutes or until frothy. (This activates the yeast.)
❷ In a large mixing bowl, combine 250 mL (1 cup) water and yeast mixture.
❸ Stir in half the all-purpose and half the whole wheat flours, and the salt. Beat vigorously about 30 strokes.
❹ Stir in remaining flour, a little at a time, first stirring with spoon, then working it in with hands to form a rough dough.
❺ Turn out onto a lightly floured work surface, countertop or bread board.
❻ Knead dough, turning with fingers and pressing with the heel of the hand about 10 minutes or until dough is smooth, satiny, elastic, and feels alive under the hands.
❼ Brush oil on bottom of clean bowl. Place dough in bowl, turn to coat dough very slightly with oil.
❽ Cover and let rise in a draft free place about 1 hour or until it is double its original size.
❾ Push down and knead again for a few minutes.
❿ Shape and form into bread, rolls, hamburger buns, pizza crust, English-style muffins and even bread sticks or combinations: e.g. 1 loaf bread, 6 English-style muffins (see recipes that follow).

French-Style Whole Wheat Bread

Preparation time: 1½ hours
Baking time: 35 to 40 minutes

Bread freezes well so while you are at it, make a double batch by simply multiplying all the ingredients by two. If you shape the loaves as I suggest, they can bake on a baking sheet and there will be no need for loaf pans. Better than that, make one or two loaves and a couple of other shapes — a pizza crust, or buns.

❶ Prepare Auntie Kay's Magic Bread dough to step 9.
❷ Sprinkle cornmeal on a lightly greased or nonstick baking sheet or jelly roll pan.
❸ With a sharp knife, cut dough into two equal portions. Shape each into a ball and let rest for 3 to 4 minutes under a towel. If necessary, lightly flour work surface to prevent dough from sticking.
❹ Form each ball into a loaf by pressing it into a 20 cm (8 in) square. Fold it in half lengthwise; pinch seam tightly to seal. Tuck ends under, pressing firmly. Place ovals on prepared pan, seam side down.
❺ Place pan in a warm place. Lightly cover with a cloth. Let rise for 30 to 45 minutes or until loaves are nearly double in size.
❻ Bake in a 190°C (375°F) oven 35 minutes or until browned and loaves sound hollow when tapped.
❼ Remove from oven. Turn loaves out, top crust up, onto wire racks to cool.

Makes 2 loaves, 9 slices each

Each serving: 1 slice
1 ☐ Starchy Choice

15 g carbohydrate   290 kilojoules
2 g protein   (68 Calories)

● **Timely Tip:** To freeze bread in any of its various shapes, first allow it to cool to room temperature. Sometimes I slice it before I freeze it. Wrap it in airtight freezer wrap, plastic wrap or foil. Seal package, label it and store it in the freezer. It will keep its fresh-baked goodness in the freezer up to 3 months. Thaw at room temperature. Frozen slices can be popped into the toaster without being thawed.

Pita Bread

Preparation time: 10 minutes
Standing: 30 minutes
Baking time: 10 to 12 minutes

For some strange reason, flipping the breads over just before baking is the trick that helps make the pocket between the two crusts of the pita bread.

❶ Prepare Auntie Kay's Magic Bread dough to step 6.
❷ With a sharp knife, cut dough into 2 equal portions. Shape each into a long roll; divide and cut into 9 equal slices. Form each into a round ball.
❸ Flatten with a rolling pin into small rounds 18 cm (7 in) in diameter and about 5 mm (1/4 in) thick.
❹ Sprinkle lightly greased or nonstick baking sheet with cornmeal.
❺ Place the flat round loaves on prepared baking sheet; cover with a towel. Let rise, about 30 minutes or until they are double in height.
❻ Preheat oven to 220°C (450°F).
❼ Turn rounds over on baking sheet.
❽ Bake in 220°C (450°F) oven for 10 to 12 minutes or until rounds are puffed and golden. Please do not open oven to peak during baking process.
❾ Remove from pan and place on wire rack to cool. Puffs will be hard and crisp when they come from oven but they flatten and crusts soften as they cool.
❿ Use within 2 days or freeze.
⓫ To use, cut or tear crosswise in half and slip finger or blunt edge of knife in between crusts to form pocket or pouch. Now the bread makes an ideal container for a sandwich filling or salad.

Makes 9 whole pita breads

Each serving: 1 pita bread
2 ◼ Starchy Choices

31 g carbohydrate   640 kilojoules
 5 g protein   (153 Calories)
 1 g fat

English Muffins

Preparation time: 20 to 25 minutes
Standing time: 30 to 40 minutes
Cooking time: 20 minutes

An oven isn't absolutely necessary for baking bread. English muffins cooked in a skillet are crusty on the outside and light on the inside.

① Prepare Auntie Kay's Magic Bread dough to step 9.
② Sprinkle work surface sparingly with cornmeal; place dough on cornmeal. Do not turn dough.
③ With a rolling pin, roll out dough about 1 cm (½ in) thick. Sprinkle top with more cornmeal.
④ Cut into 7.5 cm (3 in) rounds. Press each one out to 6 mm (⅜ in) thick.
⑤ Sprinkle bread board or counter again with cornmeal. Place rounds on surface. Cover with a towel and let rise until they are nearly double in height.
⑥ Heat a heavy nonstick skillet (an electric one is perfect) to hot.
⑦ Bake muffins, turning with a lifter, for 2 minutes on each side. Reduce heat to medium-high and bake 7 minutes longer on each side.
⑧ Remove muffins and set out on cooling rack to cool.
⑨ To use, pull muffins apart with tines of fork or the fingers. (Cutting with a knife will eliminate the wonderful taste and texture sensation of the rough peaks and valleys when they are toasted golden brown.)

One batch makes 9 muffins

Each serving: 1 English muffin
2 ☐ Starchy Choices

31 g carbohydrate   640 kilojoules
 5 g protein   (153 Calories)
 1 g fat

Scones

Preparation time: 5 minutes
Baking time: 30 minutes

Scones are very British and usually make their appearance at teatime in England. I like them instead of bread at breakfast, lunch or dinner. I also like to make the dough into one large flat cake to be cut into portions at the table. And slices are excellent toasted.

250 mL	all-purpose flour	1 cup
125 mL	whole wheat flour	½ cup
7 mL	baking powder	1½ tsp
2 mL	baking soda	½ tsp
2 mL	salt	½ tsp
125 mL	buttermilk or sour skim milk*	½ cup
1	egg	1
15 mL	melted butter	1 tbsp

❶ In a mixing bowl, combine flours, baking powder, soda and salt.
❷ In a small bowl, whisk together buttermilk, egg and butter; stir into dry ingredients just until mixed. Do not overmix.
❸ On a lightly floured surface, knead dough for 6 to 8 strokes and form into a 4 cm (1½ in) thick round biscuit.
❹ Place on a lightly greased or nonstick baking sheet. Pat down and cut slashes across the top in the form of an X.
❺ Bake in a 180°C (350°F) oven for 30 minutes or until golden brown.
❻ Cut into 8 wedges to serve.

Makes 8 servings
Each serving: 1 wedge, ⅛ of scone
1 ⬜ Starchy Choice
½ ▲ Fats & Oils Choice

16 g carbohydrate   410 kilojoules
4 g protein   (98 Calories)
2 g fat

Variations:

Cheese and Chive Scones: Add 25 mL (2 tbsp) grated Parmesan cheese and 25 mL (2 tbsp) fresh or frozen chopped chives to the dry ingredients.

Makes 8 servings

Each serving: 1 wedge, ⅛ of scone

1 ☐ Starchy Choice

½ ▲ Fats & Oils Choice

16 g carbohydrate   470 kilojoules

5 g protein   (111 Calories)

3 g fat

Raisin and Lemon Scones: Add 50 mL (¼ cup) chopped raisins and 5 mL (1 tsp) grated lemon rind to the dry ingredients.

Makes 8 servings

Each serving: 1 wedge, ⅛ of scone

1 ☐ Starchy Choice

½ ▰ Fruits & Vegetables Choice

½ ▲ Fats & Oils Choice

20 g carbohydrate   480 kilojoules

4 g protein   (114 Calories)

2 g fat

● **Timely Tip:** *To make sour skim milk, add 5 mL (1 tsp) lemon juice or vinegar to 125 mL (½ cup) skim milk. Let stand for 5 to 10 minutes at room temperature, then use.

Pizza Crust

Preparation time: 1 hour
Cooking time: 20 minutes

I like to keep a couple of these in the freezer for spur-of-the-moment cooking when the kids feel like having a pizza.

❶ Prepare Auntie Kay's Magic Bread dough to step 6.

❷ Sprinkle 2 lightly greased or nonstick pizza pans or baking sheets with cornmeal.

❸ With a knife, cut dough into 2 equal portions. Shape each into a ball and let rest for 3 to 4 minutes under a towel.

❹ With a rolling pin, flatten balls and roll each one into a round crust about 1 cm (½ in) thick. Place on pans. Press dough down in centre leaving a 2.5 cm (1 in) raised edge all around crust.

❺ Bake in a 190°C (375°F) oven for 20 minutes or until just baked and beginning to brown. (Crust will continue to bake after it is covered with filling.)

❻ Remove from oven. Cool on wire racks. Wrap and store to use for Pizzeria Pizza (recipe, p. 105). Crusts can be frozen if wrapped in foil or freezer wrap, then plastic wrap, for up to 2 months in freezer section of refrigerator.

Makes 2 pizza crusts

Each serving: ⅑ pizza crust

1 ☐ Starchy Choice

15 g carbohydrate   290 kilojoules

2 g protein   (68 Calories)

Banana Nut Muffins

Preparation time: 10 minutes
Cooking time: 20 to 25 minutes

Surprise your friends with muffin cakes. Drop the batter by the spoonful into 12 mounds on a lightly greased baking sheet. It is easier than using muffin cups. The result is muffins that look like big cookies.

250 mL	all-purpose flour	1	cup
125 mL	whole wheat flour	½	cup
15 mL	bulk granulated artificial sweetener, like SugarTwin, equivalent to 15 mL (1 tbsp) sugar	1	tbsp
7 mL	baking powder	1½	tsp
2 mL	baking soda	½	tsp
2 mL	salt	½	tsp
125 mL	buttermilk or sour skim milk*	½	cup
1	banana, mashed	1	
1	egg, lightly beaten	1	
5 mL	vanilla	1	tsp
15 mL	melted butter or margarine	1	tbsp
25 mL	chopped walnuts, optional	2	tbsp

❶ Lightly grease muffin cups, spray with low-calorie vegetable coating or line with paper muffin cups.
❷ In a bowl, combine flours, sweetener, baking powder, baking soda and salt.
❸ In a separate bowl, combine buttermilk with mashed banana, egg, vanilla and butter. Make a well in dry ingredients; pour in banana mixture and add nuts, if desired.
❹ Mix just until dry ingredients are moistened.
❺ Fill muffin cups ⅔ full.
❻ Bake in 200°C (400°F) oven for 20 minutes or until lightly browned.

Makes 12 medium muffins

Each serving: 1 muffin
1 ☐ Starchy Choice
½ ▲ Fats & Oils Choice

13 g carbohydrate   340 kilojoules
 3 g protein   (82 Calories)
 2 g fat

*See Timely Tip, p. 172

Orange Cornmeal Muffins

Preparation time: 10 minutes
Standing time: 10 minutes
Cooking time: 20 minutes

*Orange brings out the crunchy sweetness of the cornmeal.
Serve these golden gems with Chili (recipe, p. 136) or Mexican
Beans and Rice (recipe, p. 135) or as an energizing snack.*

75 mL	cornmeal	⅓ cup
125 mL	skim milk	½ cup
75 mL	orange juice	⅓ cup
15 mL	corn syrup	1 tbsp
5 mL	vanilla	1 tsp
250 mL	all-purpose flour	1 cup
15 mL	bulk granulated artificial sweetener, like SugarTwin equivalent to 15 mL (1 tbsp) sugar	1 tbsp
10 mL	baking powder	2 tsp
10 mL	grated orange rind	2 tsp
2 mL	baking soda	½ tsp
2 mL	salt	½ tsp
1	egg, lightly beaten	1
125 mL	grated carrot	½ cup
15 mL	unsalted butter or margarine, melted	1 tbsp

❶ Lightly grease muffin cups, spray with low calorie vegetable coating or line with paper muffin cups.
❷ In a bowl, combine cornmeal, skim milk, orange juice, corn syrup and vanilla; let stand for 10 minutes.
❸ In a separate bowl, combine flour, sweetener, baking powder, orange rind, soda and salt.
❹ Stir egg, carrot and butter into cornmeal mixture.
❺ Add cornmeal mixture to dry ingredients; stir just until all dry ingredients are moistened.
❻ Fill muffin cups ⅔ full.
❼ Bake in a 200°C (400°F) oven for 20 minutes or until golden brown.

Makes 12 medium muffins

Each serving: 1 muffin

1 ☐ Starchy Choice

13 g carbohydrate   290 kilojoules
2 g protein   (69 Calories)
1 g fat

Raisin Oat Bran Muffins

Preparation time: 10 minutes
Cooking time: 20 minutes

Chopping the raisins releases some of their natural sweetness and spreads them more evenly through the batter.

250 mL	all-purpose flour	1 cup
175 mL	oat bran	⅔ cup
15 mL	bulk granulated artificial sweetener, like SugarTwin, equivalent to 15 mL (1 tbsp) sugar	1 tbsp
10 mL	baking powder	2 tsp
2 mL	baking soda	½ tsp
2 mL	ground cardamom	½ tsp
2 mL	salt	½ tsp
200 mL	buttermilk or sour skim milk*	¾ cup
1	egg, lightly beaten	1
15 mL	corn oil	1 tbsp
15 mL	molasses	1 tbsp
5 mL	vanilla	1 tsp
50 mL	raisins, finely chopped	¼ cup

❶ Lightly grease muffin cups, spray with low calorie vegetable coating or line with paper muffin cups.
❷ In a bowl, combine flour, oat bran, sweetener, baking powder, baking soda, cardamom and salt.
❸ In a separate small mixing bowl, combine buttermilk, egg, corn oil, molasses and vanilla.
❹ Make a well in dry ingredients, pour in buttermilk mixture and add raisins. Mix just until dry ingredients are moistened.
❺ Fill muffin cups ⅔ full.
❻ Bake in a 200°C (400°F) oven for 20 minutes or until lightly browned.

Makes 12 medium muffins

Each serving: 1 muffin
1 ⬜ Starchy Choice
½ ▲ Fats & Oils Choice

13 g carbohydrate   340 kilojoules
3 g protein   (82 Calories)
2 g fat

● **Timely Tip:** *To sour skim milk, add 5 mL (1 tsp) lemon juice or vinegar to 200 mL (¾ cup) skim milk. Let stand for 5 to 10 minutes at room temperature, then use.

Apricot Loaf

Preparation time: 10 minutes
Standing time: 10 minutes
Baking time: 1 hour

This moist, fruity loaf mellows after being stored for a few days, so make it several days before you plan to serve it. Wrap it in plastic wrap once it has cooled, then keep it in the bread box or refrigerator. The whole loaf or portions of it freeze well. Slices, wrapped in plastic wrap and stashed in the freezer, are handy for dropping into the lunch box.

50 mL	chopped dried apricots (about 6)	¼ cup
125 mL	All Bran or 100% bran cereal	½ cup
25 mL	lightly packed brown sugar	2 tbsp
40 mL	bulk granulated artificial sweetener, like SugarTwin, equivalent to 40 mL (8 tsp) sugar	8 tsp
250 mL	skim milk	1 cup
1	egg	1
10 mL	vegetable oil	2 tsp
375 mL	all-purpose flour	1½ cups
10 mL	baking powder	2 tsp

❶ In mixing bowl, combine apricots, All Bran, sugar, sweetener and milk. Let stand about 10 minutes.
❷ Beat in egg and oil.
❸ Stir in flour and baking powder; stir until all dry ingredients are moistened.
❹ Spoon into lightly greased and floured 1.5 L (8 x 4 in) loaf pan.
❺ Bake in 190°C (375°F) oven for 1 hour or until firm to touch and tester inserted in centre comes out clean. Wrap and store for a couple of days.

Makes 1 loaf, cut into twelve 2 cm (¾ in) slices

Each serving: 1 slice
1 ▢ Starchy Choice

16 g carbohydrate   360 kilojoules
3 g protein   (85 Calories)
1 g fat

Snacking Cake

Preparation time: 10 minutes
Baking time: 30 minutes

*When the cake comes out of the oven it seems dry and firm;
however, it acts as a sponge when the syrup is poured over it.
It soaks up the liquid. You can see it swell as it becomes moist
and fluffy.*

200 mL	all-purpose flour	¾	cup
5 mL	baking powder	1	tsp
2 mL	cinnamon	½	tsp
2 mL	salt	½	tsp
1 mL	ground nutmeg	¼	tsp
50 mL	melted butter	¼	cup
75 mL	granulated sugar	⅓	cup
2	eggs	2	
50 mL	skim milk	¼	cup
5 mL	grated lemon rind	1	tsp
125 mL	chopped walnuts	½	cup
	Syrup:		
250 mL	water	1	cup
	Artificial sweetener, like SugarTwin, equivalent to 175 mL (⅔ cup) sugar		
25 mL	lemon juice	2	tbsp
1	stick (5 cm/2 in) cinnamon	1	
4	whole cloves	4	

❶ In a small bowl, combine flour, baking powder, cinnamon, salt and nutmeg.
❷ In a second larger bowl, beat together butter, sugar, eggs, skim milk and lemon rind.
❸ Stir in dry ingredients and fold in walnuts.
❹ Pour into a lightly greased 20 cm (8 in) square baking pan.
❺ Bake in a 180°C (350°F) oven for 25 to 30 minutes or until a tester inserted in the centre comes out clean. Cool in pan.
❻ Syrup: In a saucepan, combine water, sweetener, lemon juice, cinnamon stick and cloves. Bring to a boil.
❼ Prick cake in many places with a fork and pour syrup over cake. Allow to sit 5 to 10 minutes for cake to absorb syrup.
❽ Cut into pieces and serve.
❾ Store cake, covered, in the refrigerator.

Makes 20 snack-size pieces, 9 dessert-size pieces

Each snack-size serving: ¹⁄₂₀ of cake

½	☐ Starchy Choice	8 g carbohydrate	360 kilojoules
1	▲ Fats & Oils Choice	2 g protein	(85 Calories)
		5 g fat	

Each dessert-size serving: ¹⁄₉ of cake

1	☐ Starchy Choice	17 g carbohydrate	730 kilojoules
2	▲ Fats & Oils Choices	4 g protein	(174 Calories)
		10 g fat	

Apple Spice Squares

Preparation time: 15 minutes
Cooking time: 50 minutes
Standing time: 15 minutes

Tangy apple butter, sandwiched between crumb layers, makes these squares sweet and chewy. One of the best — my family's favorite.

125	mL	all-purpose flour	½ cup
125	mL	quick-cooking rolled oats	½ cup
5	mL	baking powder	1 tsp
50	mL	unsalted margarine or butter	¼ cup
50	mL	water	¼ cup
1		egg, separated	1
		Artificial sweetener, like SugarTwin, equivalent to 125 mL (½ cup) sugar	
5	mL	vanilla	1 tsp
250	mL	Apple Butter (recipe, p. 200)	1 cup
1	mL	cream of tartar	¼ tsp
15	mL	brown sugar	1 tbsp
125	mL	unsweetened shredded coconut	½ cup
125	mL	bran flakes, crushed	½ cup

❶ Lightly grease a 20 cm (8 in) square cake pan.
❷ In a bowl, combine flour, rolled oats and baking powder. With a pastry blender or two knives, cut in margarine until mixture is crumbly.
❸ In a small bowl, beat together water, egg yolk, and sweetener. Stir into crumbly dry mixture. Press onto bottom of cake pan.
❹ Stir vanilla into Apple Butter; spread over crumb layer in pan.
❺ In a bowl, beat egg white with cream of tartar until frothy. Add sugar gradually and beat until soft peaks form. Fold in coconut and bran flakes. Spread carefully and evenly over Apple Butter layer. Press down lightly with a fork.
❻ Bake in a 180°C (350°F) oven for 30 minutes or until top is lightly browned. Cool and cut into 25 squares.

Makes 25 squares, each 4 x 4 cm (1½ in)

Each serving: 2 squares
1 ☐ Starchy Choice
1 ▲ Fats & Oils Choice

13 g carbohydrate   440 kilojoules
2 g protein   (105 Calories)
5 g fat

Coconut Orange Hermits

Preparation time: 10 minutes
Baking time: 15 minutes

Hermits are soft cookies that look like little rugged hills. Fruit, nuts and spices are usually mixed into the batter.

175 mL	all-purpose flour	⅔ cup
175 mL	whole wheat flour	⅔ cup
7 mL	baking powder	1½ tsp
50 mL	margarine or butter	¼ cup
15 mL	grated orange rind (1 small orange)	1 tbsp
50 mL	shredded unsweetened coconut	¼ cup
25 mL	currants or chopped raisins	2 tbsp
25 mL	lightly packed brown sugar	2 tbsp
1	egg	1
50 mL	orange juice	¼ cup
	Artificial sweetener, like SugarTwin, equivalent to 30 mL (6 tsp) sugar	

❶ In a mixing bowl, combine flours and baking powder.
❷ With a pastry blender or two knives, cut in margarine to form a crumbly mixture.
❸ Stir in orange rind, coconut, raisins and brown sugar.
❹ Whisk egg with orange juice and sweetener. Stir into flour mixture; mix until all ingredients are just moistened.
❺ Drop 15 mL (1 tbsp) batter at a time onto lightly greased or nonstick baking sheets about 4 cm (1½ in) apart.
❻ Bake in a 190°C (375°F) oven for 12 to 15 minutes or until lightly browned.

Makes 24 Hermits

Each serving: 2 Hermits

1 ☐ Starchy Choice
1 ▲ Fats & Oils Choice

14 g carbohydrate
2 g protein
5 g fat

460 kilojoules
(109 Calories)

Crisp Grainy Wafers

Preparation time: 10 minutes
Baking time: 30 minutes

The two-step process of first baking these cookies, then drying them out, guarantees their crispness.

125 mL	all-purpose flour	½ cup
125 mL	whole wheat flour	½ cup
10 mL	baking powder	2 tsp
50 mL	margarine or butter	¼ cup
250 mL	bran flakes	1 cup
125 mL	quick-cooking rolled oats	½ cup
50 mL	shredded unsweetened coconut	¼ cup
50 mL	chopped nuts	¼ cup
25 mL	lightly packed brown sugar	2 tbsp
1	egg	1
125 mL	water	½ cup
5 mL	vanilla	1 tsp
	Liquid artificial sweetener, like SugarTwin, equivalent to 40 mL (8 tsp) sugar	
2 mL	cinnamon	½ tsp

❶ In a mixing bowl, combine flours and baking powder.
❷ With a pastry blender or two knives, cut in margarine to form a crumbly mixture.
❸ Stir in bran flakes, rolled oats, coconut, nuts and brown sugar.
❹ Whisk egg with water, vanilla, sweetener and cinnamon. Stir into flour mixture; mix just until all ingredients are moistened.
❺ Drop 5 mL (1 tsp) batter at a time onto lightly greased or nonstick baking sheet 4 cm (1½ in) apart.
❻ Bake in a 190°C (375°F) oven for 12 minutes or until lightly browned.
❼ After all the cookies have baked, arrange them in layers on a single cookie sheet and return cookies to oven; immediately turn off heat. Allow cookies to stay in for 10 to 15 minutes to dry and crisp. Store in a covered container, with loose-fitting lid.

Makes 60 cookies

Each serving: 4 cookies

1 ▢ Starchy Choice
1 ▲ Fats & Oils Choice

12 g carbohydrate   420 kilojoules
2 g protein   (101 Calories)
5 g fat

Pecan Crisps

Preparation time: 10 minutes
Cooking time: 50 minutes
Standing time: 10 minutes

Everyone loves these cookies. They are light and airy with a nutty crispness.

2		egg whites	2	
	Pinch	cream of tartar		Pinch
50	mL	brown sugar, lightly packed	¼	cup
2	mL	vanilla	½	tsp
75	mL	chopped pecans	⅓	cup
250	mL	rice cereal	1	cup

❶ Line baking sheets with brown paper.
❷ Beat egg whites with cream of tartar until soft peaks form. Add sugar gradually, then vanilla; beat until stiff peaks form.
❸ Fold in pecans and rice cereal.
❹ Drop 15 mL (1 tbsp) batter at a time 5 cm (2 in) apart onto prepared baking sheets.
❺ Bake in a 160°C (325°F) oven for 20 minutes or until firm.
❻ Turn off oven and leave cookies in for ½ hour longer to dry. Remove from oven and cool.
❼ Peel cookies from paper when cooled.

Makes 18 cookies

Each serving: 3 cookies
1 ☐ Starchy Choice
1 ▲ Fats & Oils Choice

12 g carbohydrate   420 kilojoules
2 g protein   (101 Calories)
5 g fat

Butterscotch Peanut Cookies

Preparation time: 15 minutes
Cooking time: 18 minutes

Flattening each cookie with a fork ensures a crispy texture. Use chunky peanut butter for extra crunch and real peanut flavor.

250 mL	quick-cooking rolled oats	1 cup
250 mL	all-purpose flour	1 cup
125 mL	whole wheat flour	½ cup
10 mL	baking powder	2 tsp
175 mL	chunky peanut butter	⅔ cup
125 mL	unsalted butter or margarine	½ cup
125 mL	water	½ cup
10 mL	vinegar	2 tsp
1	egg yolk	1
	Artificial sweetener, like SugarTwin, equivalent to 175 mL (⅔ cup) sugar	
5 mL	vanilla	1 tsp

❶ In a bowl, combine rolled oats, flours and baking powder. With pastry blender or 2 knives, cut in peanut butter and margarine until mixture is crumbly.

❷ In a small bowl, beat together water, vinegar, egg yolk, sweetener and vanilla. Stir into crumbly dry mixture; mix well.

❸ Form 15 mL (1 tbsp) batter at a time into small balls. Place balls 2.5 cm (1 in) apart on a nonstick baking sheet.

❹ With the tines of a fork, flatten each ball by pressing in several directions until each cookie is a circle 6 cm (2½ in) wide.

❺ Bake in a 180°C (350°F) oven for 15 to 18 minutes or until lightly browned. Let cool.

❻ Store in a tightly covered cookie jar or container.

Makes 60 cookies

Each serving: 2 cookies
½ ☐ Starchy Choice
1 ▲ Fats & Oils Choice

7 g carbohydrate
2 g protein
6 g fat

380 kilojoules
(90 Calories)

Double Chocolate Oatmeal Cookies

Preparation time: 15 minutes
Cooking time: 18 minutes

For real chocolate lovers — a crunchy cookie under the easiest frosting ever!

250 mL	quick-cooking rolled oats	1	cup
250 mL	all-purpose flour	1	cup
250 mL	whole wheat flour	1	cup
25 mL	dry unsweetened cocoa	2	tbsp
10 mL	baking powder	2	tsp
125 mL	unsalted margarine or butter	½	cup
125 mL	water	½	cup
2	egg yolks	2	
	Liquid artificial sweetener, like SugarTwin, equivalent to 250 mL (1 cup) sugar		
5 mL	almond extract	1	tsp
125 mL	chocolate chips	½	cup

❶ In a bowl, combine oats, flours, cocoa and baking powder. With a pastry blender or 2 knives, cut in margarine until mixture is crumbly.

❷ In a small bowl, beat together water, egg yolks, sweetener and almond extract. Stir into crumbly mixture; mix well.

❸ Form 15 mL (1 tbsp) batter at a time into small balls. Place balls 2.5 cm (1 in) apart on a nonstick baking sheet.

❹ With the tines of a fork, flatten each ball by pressing in several directions until each cookie is a circle 6 cm (2½ in) wide.

❺ Bake in a 180°C (350°F) oven for 15 to 18 minutes or until lightly browned.

❻ As soon as cookies are removed from the oven, immediately place 2 chocolate chips in the centre of each cookie. Let stand 1 minute. With the back of a spoon, spread or swirl chocolate chips (which are hot and soft) on top of each cookie to partly frost each cookie. Let cool.

❼ Store in a tightly covered cookie jar or container.

Makes 60 cookies

Each serving: 3 cookies

1	☐ Starchy Choice	15 g carbohydrate	570 kilojoules
1½	▲ Fats & Oils Choice	3 g protein	(135 Calories)
		7 g fat	

Recipe	Food Choices Per Serving	Energy Per Serving		
		kilojoules	Calories	
Auntie Kay's Magic Bread (French-Style Whole Wheat Bread)	1 ☐ Starchy	290	68	p. 164
Pita Bread	2 ☐ Starchy	640	153	p. 166
English Muffins	2 ☐ Starchy	640	153	p. 167
Scones	1 ☐ Starchy; ½ ▲ Fats & Oils	410	98	p. 168
Cheese and Chive Scones	1 ☐ Starchy; ½ ▲ Fats & Oils	470	111	p. 168
Raisin and Lemon Scones	1 ☐ Starchy; ½ ▲ Fats & Oils; ½ ◢ Fruits & Vegetables	480	114	p. 169
Pizza Crust	1 ☐ Starchy	290	68	p. 169
Banana Nut Muffins	1 ☐ Starchy; ½ ▲ Fats & Oils	340	82	p. 170
Orange Cornmeal Muffins	1 ☐ Starchy	290	69	p. 171
Raisin Oat Bran Muffins	1 ☐ Starchy; ½ ▲ Fats & Oils	340	82	p. 172
Apricot Loaf	1 ☐ Starchy	360	85	p. 173
Snacking Cake — snack size serving — dessert size serving	½ ☐ Starchy; 1 ▲ Fats & Oils 1 ☐ Starchy; 2 ▲ Fats & Oils	360 730	85 174	p. 174
Apple Spice Squares	1 ☐ Starchy; 1 ▲ Fats & Oils	440	105	p. 176
Coconut Orange Hermits	1 ☐ Starchy; 1 ▲ Fats & Oils	460	109	p. 177
Crispy Grainy Wafers	1 ☐ Starchy; 1 ▲ Fats & Oils	420	101	p. 178
Pecan Crisps	1 ☐ Starchy; 1 ▲ Fats & Oils	420	101	p. 179
Butterscotch Peanut Cookies	½ ☐ Starchy; 1 ▲ Fats & Oils	380	90	p. 180
Double Chocolate Oatmeal Cookies	1 ☐ Starchy; 1½ ▲ Fats & Oils	570	135	p. 181

Notes

Delicious Desserts

Some desserts are dazzling like cheesecake and chocolate soufflé. Others are simple like a gelatin dessert or a piece of fruit. Dazzling or simple, they add the finishing touch to a meal.

For that final touch to be perfect, choose a dessert that contrasts with the main part of the meal. If the main course is a cold salad, have a creamy custard or hot rice pudding for dessert. If a roast with its trimmings is featured, then a light fruit dessert is refreshing.

Desserts in this collection will suit any of your mealtime requirements. And most of them will fit in as special snacks on their own, especially if you have a bit of a sweet tooth. The choice is yours. Always remember to take note of the Food Choices and either choose desserts that round out your meal plan or plan your meal so you can have the dessert of your choice.

◀ From top clockwise:
Chocolate Mousse,
Strawberry Rhubarb Pie,
Snow Gelatin

Coconut Rice Pudding

Preparation time: 10 minutes

Creamy rice combined with the crunch of coconut makes a delectable and satisfying finishing touch to a meal.

250 mL	cooked short grain rice	**1**	**cup**
125 mL	skim milk	**½**	**cup**
	Artificial sweetener, like SugarTwin, equivalent to 30 mL (6 tsp) sugar		
5 mL	vanilla	**1**	**tsp**
25 mL	shredded unsweetened coconut	**1**	**tbsp**

❶ In a saucepan, combine cooked rice, skim milk, artificial sweetener, vanilla and shredded coconut.
❷ Bring to a boil; reduce heat and simmer, stirring occasionally, for 5 minutes, or until most of moisture evaporates, rice kernels stick together and mixture is creamy.

Makes 250 mL (1 cup), 2 servings

Each serving: 125 mL (½ cup)

1 ☐ Starchy Choice	22 g carbohydrate	470 kilojoules
1 ◆ Milk Choice (skim)	4 g protein	(113 Calories)
	1 g fat	

● **Timely Tip:** Cooked rice can be frozen in 250 mL (1 cup) portions in small plastic freezer bags. Push all the air out of the bag of rice, close and secure it with twist-ties. Label it with name, date and instructions for use. It will keep for up to 3 months. To defrost quickly, place the rice in a sieve and pour boiling water over it. When you are in the mood for rice pudding, it sure is handy to have a little rice cooked and ready.

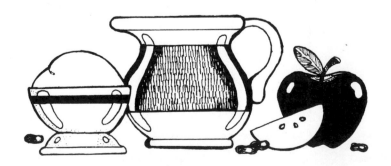

Apple Raisin Rice Pudding

Preparation time: 10 minutes

This creamy rice pudding with plump raisins and juicy apple is a good old-fashioned, family favorite. When the rice is precooked it takes only about 10 minutes to make it.

500 mL	cooked short grain rice	2 cups
250 mL	skim milk	1 cup
	Artificial sweetener, like SugarTwin, equivalent to 60 mL (12 tsp) sugar	
50 mL	raisins	¼ cup
5 mL	vanilla	1 tsp
1 mL	ground cinnamon	¼ tsp
1 mL	ground nutmeg	¼ tsp
1	apple	1
1 mL	ascorbic acid color keeper	¼ tsp

❶ In a saucepan, combine cooked rice, skim milk, sweetener, raisins, vanilla, cinnamon and nutmeg. Bring to a boil; reduce heat and simmer, stirring occasionally, for 5 minutes or until most of moisture evaporates and mixture is creamy.

❷ Core and shred apple and sprinkle with ascorbic acid color keeper.

❸ Stir apple into rice mixture. Cook for 2 to 3 minutes longer or until apple is soft.

❹ Spoon into serving dish or dessert dishes. Serve warm or chilled.

Makes 750 mL (3 cups), 6 servings

Each serving: 125 mL (½ cup)

1 ☐ Starchy Choice	22 g carbohydrate	400 kilojoules
1 ◆ Milk Choice (skim)	2 g protein	(96 Calories)

Vanilla Pudding

Preparation time: 15 minutes

Pudding gives soup or salad suppers the perfect finishing touch.

500 mL	2% or skim milk	2 cups
75 mL	cornstarch	⅓ cup
2	egg yolks OR 1 whole egg	2
75 mL	bulk granulated artificial sweetener, like SugarTwin, equivalent to 75 mL (⅓ cup) sugar	⅓ cup
10 mL	vanilla	2 tsp

❶ In a heavy saucepan, combine 125 mL (½ cup) of the milk and cornstarch; mix well. Add remaining milk. Place over medium heat and cook, stirring, until mixture comes to a boil; reduce heat and simmer for 2 minutes. Remove from heat.
❷ In a bowl, beat egg yolks or whole egg with a fork; add a small amount (125 mL/½ cup) of the hot mixture to beaten egg, stirring until smooth; return immediately to hot mixture, stirring constantly. (The hot mixture will cook the egg.)
❸ Stir in sweetener and vanilla.
❹ Pour 125 mL (½ cup) into each of 4 dessert dishes. Cover with plastic wrap to prevent skin from forming on top of pudding. Cool to room temperature or chill in refrigerator.

Makes 500 mL (2 cups), 4 servings

Each serving: 125 mL (½ cup)

½ ☐ Starchy Choice	18 g carbohydrate	520 kilojoules
1½ ◆ Milk Choices (2%)	6 g protein	(123 Calories)
	3 g fat	

Variation:

Chocolate Pudding: In place of the cornstarch in the above recipe, use 50 mL (¼ cup) each of cornstarch and dry unsweetened cocoa.

Calculations as above

Lemon Pudding

Preparation time: 10 minutes
Cooking time: 5 minutes

A tart pudding like this hits the spot after a main course of fish or poultry.

500 mL	water	2 cups
75 mL	cornstarch	⅓ cup
2	egg yolks OR 1 whole egg	2
75 mL	bulk granulated artificial sweetener, like SugarTwin, equivalent to 75 mL (⅓ cup) sugar	⅓ cup
50 mL	lemon juice	¼ cup

❶ In a heavy saucepan, combine 125 mL (½ cup) of the water and cornstarch; mix well. Add remaining water. Place over medium heat and cook, stirring, until mixture comes to a boil; reduce heat and simmer for 2 minutes. Remove from heat.
❷ In a bowl, beat egg yolks with a fork; add a small amount (125 mL/½ cup) of the hot mixture to beaten egg, stirring until smooth. Return immediately to hot mixture, stirring constantly. (The hot mixture will cook the egg.)
❸ Stir in sweetener and lemon juice.
❹ Pour 125 mL (½ cup) into each of 4 dessert dishes. Cover with plastic wrap to prevent skin from forming on top of pudding. Cool to room temperature or chill in refrigerator.

Makes 4 servings

Each serving: 125 mL (½ cup)

1 ☐ Starchy Choice	12 g carbohydrate 260 kilojoules
	1 g protein (61 Calories)
	1 g fat

Spiced Apple Pudding

Preparation time: 10 minutes
Cooking time: 5 minutes

My aunt made a pudding like this when I was a kid so I felt there was something really special and novel about this spicy apple one.

500 mL	unsweetened apple juice	2 cups
75 mL	cornstarch	⅓ cup
2	egg yolks OR 1 whole egg	2
75 mL	bulk granulated artificial sweetener, like SugarTwin, equivalent to 75 mL (⅓ cup) sugar	⅓ cup
2 mL	ground cinnamon	½ tsp

❶ In a heavy saucepan, combine 125 mL (½ cup) apple juice and cornstarch; mix well. Add remaining apple juice. Place over medium heat and cook, stirring, until mixture comes to a boil; reduce heat and simmer for 2 minutes. Remove from heat.
❷ In a bowl, beat egg yolks with a fork; add a small amount (125 mL/½ cup) of the hot mixture to beaten egg, stirring until smooth. Return immediately to hot mixture, stirring constantly. (The hot mixture will cook the egg.)
❸ Stir in sweetener and cinnamon.
❹ Pour 125 mL (½ cup) into each of 4 dessert dishes. Cover with plastic wrap to prevent skin from forming on top of pudding. Cool to room temperature or chill in refrigerator.

Makes 4 servings

Each serving: 125 mL (½ cup)

1 ☐ Starchy Choice	26 g carbohydrate	490 kilojoules
1 ▨ Fruits & Vegetables Choice	1 g protein	(117 Calories)
	1 g fat	

Variation:

Spiced Pineapple Pudding: In place of apple juice, use unsweetened pineapple juice.

Calculations as above

Snow Gelatin

Preparation time: 10 minutes
Standing time: 30 minutes
Chilling time: 2 to 4 hours

This light dessert is adapted from the cuisine of Japan. The Japanese always decorate it with a pretty garnish of colorful fruit.

1	envelope unflavored gelatin	1
250 mL	water	1 cup
	Artificial sweetener, like SugarTwin, equivalent to 125 mL (½ cup) sugar	
25 mL	fresh lime or lemon juice	2 tbsp
5 mL	vanilla	1 tsp
2	egg whites	2
6	strawberries or orange slices	6

❶ In a small saucepan, sprinkle gelatin over water and let stand for 5 minutes to soften. Place over low heat and stir until gelatin dissolves. Stir in sweetener, lime juice and vanilla.
❷ Chill in the refrigerator about 25 to 30 minutes or until partially set and the consistency of raw egg white.
❸ Beat egg whites until stiff peaks form. Fold into gelatin mixture.
❹ Pour into a 20 cm (8 in) square pan or a 1 L (4 cup) mold.
❺ Chill in refrigerator for 3 to 4 hours or until set.
❻ Cut gelatin in pan into 6 squares. Remove with spatula to dessert plates. Garnish each with a strawberry cut in slices or an orange slice cut in half. (If gelatin is in a mold, unmold it onto a plate and garnish attractively with strawberry or orange slices.)

Makes 750 mL (3 cups), 6 servings

Each serving: 125 mL (½ cup)

1 **++** Extra

2 g carbohydrate   70 kilojoules
2 g protein   (16 Calories)

Grape Chiffon

Preparation time: 30 minutes
Chilling time: 3 hours

For variations of this light cool dessert, unsweetened apricot or prune juice can be used in place of the grape juice without changing the choice and nutrient value.

1	envelope unflavored gelatin	1
375 mL	unsweetened grape juice	1½ cups
10 mL	lemon juice	2 tsp
	Artificial sweetener, like SugarTwin, equivalent to 30 mL (6 tsp) sugar	
5 mL	vanilla	1 tsp
2	egg whites	2

❶ In a small cup or measure, sprinkle gelatin over 125 mL (½ cup) of the juice; let stand for 5 minutes to soften.
❷ Place cup or measure in a pan of boiling water; stir until gelatin dissolves completely.
❸ In a medium bowl, combine remaining grape juice, lemon juice, sweetener and vanilla. Stir in dissolved gelatin.
❹ Chill in refrigerator for about 20 minutes or until the consistency of raw egg white and partially set.
❺ Beat egg whites until stiff peaks form. Fold about one-third of egg whites into gelatin mixture, then fold this mixture back into the remaining egg whites until evenly textured.
❻ Return to refrigerator to chill at least 2 hours or until set.

Makes 750 mL (3 cups), 6 servings

Each serving: 125 mL (½ cup)
1 ▰ Fruits & Vegetables Choice

11 g carbohydrate   220 kilojoules
2 g protein   (52 Calories)

Strawberry Rhubarb Pie

Preparation time: 20 minutes
Baking time: 40 minutes

Few Spring desserts are as luscious as this one. However, if it's not Spring and you want a delicious fruit pie, make it using frozen sliced rhubarb and frozen unsweetened strawberries.

	Crust	
200 mL	all-purpose flour	¾ cup
125 mL	whole wheat flour	½ cup
1 mL	salt	¼ tsp
45 mL	margarine or corn oil	3 tbsp
45 mL	ice water	3 tbsp
	Filling	
500 mL	sliced fresh or frozen unsweetened rhubarb (2.5 cm/1 in pieces)	2 cups
250 mL	fresh or frozen unsweetened strawberries, sliced	1 cup
50 mL	all-purpose flour	¼ cup
250 mL	bulk granulated artificial sweetener, like SugarTwin, equivalent to 250 mL (1 cup) sugar	1 cup
50 mL	unsweetened desiccated coconut	¼ cup

❶ **Crust:** In a bowl, combine flours and salt.
❷ With a pastry blender or 2 knives, cut in margarine until mixture is crumbly. Add the water gradually, stirring with a fork until mixture is moist but still crumbly.
❸ Press onto the bottom and sides of a 23 cm (9 in) pie plate with fingers, making sure pastry evenly covers both bottom and sides of the pie pan.
❹ **Filling:** In the same bowl, combine rhubarb and strawberries. Sprinkle with flour and sweetener. Toss gently.
❺ Spoon into prepared pie crust; spread evenly.
❻ Bake in a 220°C (425°F) oven for 30 minutes.
❼ Remove from oven. Sprinkle evenly with coconut; return to oven and continue to bake 10 minutes longer or until fruit is tender and top is golden brown.

Makes 1 pie, 6 servings

Each serving: ⅙ of pie
1 ☐ Starchy Choice
1 ▨ Fruits & Vegetables Choice
1 ▲ Fats & Oils Choice

26 g carbohydrate   750 kilojoules
  3 g protein   (179 Calories)
  7 g fat

Chocolate Layered Pudding

Preparation time: 10 minutes
Cooking time: 30 minutes

*As this rich tasting, chocolaty mixture bakes, three layers form
— a smooth bottom layer, a creamy middle one, and a foamy
light one on top. It is fun to eat out of the dish in which it
is baked.*

1	egg, separated	1
10 mL	granulated sugar	2 tsp
10 mL	all-purpose flour	2 tsp
	Artificial sweetener, like SugarTwin, equivalent to 30 mL (6 tsp) sugar	
15 mL	dry unsweetened cocoa	1 tbsp
125 mL	skim milk	½ cup
5 mL	vanilla	1 tsp
Pinch	cream of tartar	Pinch

❶ In a small bowl, whisk egg yolk, sugar, flour, sweetener and
cocoa. Stir in milk and vanilla.
❷ In separate bowl, beat egg white and cream of tartar until
stiff peaks form. Fold into egg yolk mixture.
❸ Pour pudding into small 200 mL (¾ cup) custard cups.
❹ Set custard cups in pan; pour in hot water to reach 2.5 cm
(1 in) up sides of cups.
❺ Bake in a 160°C (325°F) oven for 30 minutes.
❻ Serve warm or cold.

Makes 2 servings

Each serving: 1 pudding, 200 mL (¾ cup)

1½ ◆ Milk Choices (2%)   11 g carbohydrate   400 kilojoules
    OR   6 g protein   (95 Calories)
1 ⊘ Protein Choice   3 g fat
1 ◧ Fruits & Vegetables Choice

Chocolate Mousse

Preparation time: 15 minutes
Standing time: 2 hours

Rich and creamy, this smooth mousse is a perfect make-ahead dessert for a special dinner. To make sure the color and texture are even throughout, fold in egg whites carefully and completely.

250 mL	evaporated skim milk	1	cup
50 mL	dry unsweetened cocoa	¼	cup
2	eggs, separated	2	
5 mL	almond extract or vanilla	1	tsp
	Artificial sweetener, like SugarTwin, equivalent to 50 mL (¼ cup) sugar		
Pinch	cream of tartar		Pinch
5 mL	granulated sugar	1	tsp
	Strawberries, raspberries or whipped topping		

❶ In a medium saucepan, whisk together milk and cocoa until there are no dry lumps of cocoa.
❷ Place over medium heat. Bring to a boil; reduce heat and cook over low heat, stirring frequently, about 7 minutes or until smooth and slightly thickened. Remove from heat.
❸ Beat egg yolks with a fork; stir 125 mL (½ cup) of the hot mixture into beaten yolks, stirring until smooth; immediately return to chocolate mixture, stirring well. (It should thicken some if you work quickly before chocolate mixture cools.) Stir in almond extract and sweetener.
❹ Pour into medium bowl; cover and chill for 1 hour.
❺ Beat egg whites and cream of tartar until soft peaks form. Add sugar and beat until stiff.
❻ Stir one-quarter of beaten egg whites into cooled chocolate mixture to lighten it, then fold in remaining stiffly beaten egg whites until there are no white streaks.
❼ Spoon into small parfait glasses or cups. Cover and chill for at least 2 hours. (Will keep refrigerated up to 3 days.)
❽ Garnish each with a strawberry, a few raspberries or dollop of whipped topping.

Makes 750 mL (3 cups), 6 servings

Each serving: 125 mL (½ cup)

1 ◆ Milk Choice (homo)	5 g carbohydrate	300 kilojoules
OR	4 g protein	(72 Calories)
1 ◆ Milk Choice (skim)	4 g fat	
1 ▲ Fats & Oils Choice		

Chocolate Mousse Soufflé

Preparation time: 20 minutes
Standing time: 4 hours

Gelatin gives the mousse a little more body. Dusting with shaved chocolate gives it an elegant touch.

1	envelope unflavored gelatin	1
75 mL	unsweetened orange juice	⅓ cup
250 mL	skim milk	1 cup
50 mL	dry unsweetened cocoa	¼ cup
2	eggs, separated	2
5 mL	vanilla	1 tsp
	Artificial sweetener, like SugarTwin, equivalent to 50 mL (¼ cup) sugar	
Pinch	cinnamon	Pinch
Pinch	cream of tartar	Pinch
10 mL	grated semisweet chocolate (½ square)	2 tsp
	Whipped topping, optional	

❶ In small bowl or cup, sprinkle gelatin over orange juice and let stand for 5 minutes to soften.

❷ In saucepan, whisk together milk and cocoa until there are no dry lumps of cocoa. Place over medium heat. Bring to a boil; reduce heat and cook over low heat, stirring frequently, about 7 minutes or until smooth and slightly thickened. Remove from heat.

❸ Beat egg yolks with a fork; stir about 125 mL (½ cup) of the hot mixture into beaten yolks, stirring until smooth. Immediately return this egg yolk mixture to the chocolate mixture, stirring well. (It should thicken some if you work quickly before chocolate mixture cooks.)

❹ Stir in gelatin until it dissolves, then add vanilla, sweetener and cinnamon; mix well.

❺ Pour into medium bowl. Cover and chill in refrigerator about 30 minutes or until partially set (the consistency of unbeaten egg white).

❻ Beat egg whites with cream of tartar until stiff peaks form.

❼ Stir one-quarter of the beaten egg whites into partially set chocolate mixture, then fold in remaining stiffly beaten egg whites until there are no white streaks.

8 Spoon into straight-sided soufflé dish or mold. Chill about 4 hours or until set.

9 Unmold onto serving plate. Garnish with shredded chocolate and whipped topping, if desired.

Makes 6 servings

Each serving: 200 mL (¾ cup)

1 ◆ Milk Choice (homo)	7 g carbohydrate 320 kilojoules
OR	5 g protein (75 Calories)
1 ◆ Milk Choice (skim)	3 g fat
½ ▲ Fats & Oils Choice	

Chocolate Fondue

Preparation time: 20 minutes
Cooking time: 10 minutes

When you want a fun dessert or special snack to enjoy with friends, make this fondue. They will all join you in the fun of dipping and creating their own treat.

	Chocolate Sauce	
175 mL	dry unsweetened cocoa	⅔ cup
1 mL	cinnamon	¼ tsp
250 mL	skim milk	1 cup
2 mL	vanilla or almond extract	½ tsp
125 mL	bulk granulated artificial sweetener, like SugarTwin, equivalent to 125 mL (½ cup) sugar	½ cup
	Dippers	
1	apple, cored and cut in bite-size chunks	1
1	banana	1
250 mL	seedless green grapes	1 cup
150 mL	unsweetened pineapple chunks	⅔ cup
125 mL	bran flakes, crushed	½ cup
50 mL	chopped walnuts	¼ cup
50 mL	chopped, shredded unsweetened coconut	¼ cup

❶ In a heavy saucepan, combine cocoa, cinnamon and milk; stir or whisk until there are no dry lumps of cocoa. Stir and cook over medium heat until mixture comes to a boil. Reduce heat; boil gently, stirring often, for 5 minutes or until mixture is thick and smooth. Cool slightly.

❷ Stir in vanilla and sweetener.

❸ Pour into a small enameled fondue pot or heatproof ceramic bowl. Set on holder over a candle or source of heat to keep warm.

❹ In small dishes, place fruits, crushed cereal, walnuts and coconut around fondue pot.

❺ Provide each diner with long bamboo or wooden picks or fondue forks. Each person pierces a chunk of fruit and dips it into the fondue, then into one of the accompaniments, if desired, and then enjoys.

Makes 8 servings

Each serving: ⅛ of fruit, 50 mL (¼ cup) sauce

2 ▨ Fruits & Vegetables Choices	19 g carbohydrate	520 kilojoules
1 ▲ Fats & Oils Choice	3 g protein	(124 Calories)
	4 g fat	

Apple Clafouti

Preparation time: 10 minutes
Baking time: 30 minutes

Inspiration for this country-style dessert came from a classic French Clafouti I have been making for years. It is best described as a light, fruit-filled pancake.

2	eggs	2
125 mL	skim milk	½ cup
	Artificial sweetener, like SugarTwin, equivalent to 30 mL (6 tsp) sugar	
15 mL	all-purpose flour	1 tbsp
5 mL	almond extract	1 tsp
3	medium apples, peeled, cored and sliced	3
1 mL	cinnamon	½ tsp
Pinch	ground ginger	Pinch

❶ In a bowl, combine eggs, milk, sweetener, flour and almond extract; mix well.
❷ Arrange sliced apples in the bottom of a 20 cm (8 in) round or square nonstick baking dish. Sprinkle with cinnamon and ginger.
❸ Pour egg mixture over apples.
❹ Bake in a 180°C (350°F) oven for 30 to 35 minutes or until set and tester, inserted halfway between centre and edge of dish, comes out clean. Cool.
❺ To serve, invert on serving plate, if desired, or spoon onto dessert plates from baking dish.

Makes 6 servings

Each serving: ⅙ of dessert
½ 🟦 Protein Choice
1 ⬛ Fruits & Vegetables Choice

11 g carbohydrate   310 kilojoules
  3 g protein   (74 Calories)
  2 g fat

Variation:

Peach Clafouti or Pear Clafouti: Substitute 6 peach or pear halves (fresh or canned in their own juice and drained) for the apples.

Calculations as above

Apple Butter

Preparation time: 5 minutes
Cooking time: 15 minutes

This sauce is so thick and tasty, it makes a scrumptious spread for toast or even French toast.

4	small unpeeled apples, cored	4
	Juice and pulp of half an orange	
2 mL	ground cinnamon	½ tsp
1 mL	ground cardamom	¼ tsp
	Artificial sweetener, like SugarTwin, equivalent to 10 mL (2 tsp) sugar	

❶ Finely chop apple pieces.
❷ In a cold saucepan, combine apples, orange pulp and juice, cinnamon and cardamom. Bring to a boil over medium heat; stir well, reduce heat, and simmer, covered, for 5 minutes.
❸ Remove cover and continue to simmer, stirring, until no juice shows on the bottom of the pan. Remove from heat before any browning takes place.
❹ Stir in sweetener.

Makes 250 mL (1 cup) Apple Butter, 4 servings

Each serving: 50 mL (¼ cup)
1 ◻ Fruits & Vegetables Choice   12 g carbohydrate   200 kilojoules
                                                           (48 Calories)

OR

Each serving: 15 mL (1 tbsp)
1 ➕ Extra   3 g carbohydrate   50 kilojoules
                                                           (12 Calories)

Vanilla Creme Custard

Preparation time: 10 minutes
Cooking time: 35 minutes
Standing time: 1 hour

Warm or cold baked custard is one of my comfort foods. It feels nice and tastes good.

2	eggs	2	
375 mL	skim milk	1½	cups
	Artificial sweetener, like SugarTwin, equivalent to 30 mL (6 tsp) sugar		
5 mL	vanilla	1	tsp
2	Double Chocolate Oatmeal cookies (recipe, p. 181)	2	

1 In a bowl, with a whisk or hand beater, gently beat eggs until just mixed. Stir in milk, sweetener and vanilla.
2 Pour into a 750 mL (3 cup) ovenproof baking dish or casserole. Cover top with foil.
3 Place in a larger pan. Pour in hot water to reach 5 cm (2 in) up sides of baking dish.
4 Bake in a 180°C (350°F) oven for 35 minutes or until tester, inserted between centre and outside edge, comes out clean.
5 Cool for 10 minutes, then cover and refrigerate until serving time. (Custard can be made 1 day ahead.)
6 Crush cookies to make crumbs. Sprinkle over custard.
7 Place under broiler for 1 to 2 minutes to toast crumbs. Remove.
8 Serve in dessert dishes in the kitchen or at the table.

Makes 4 servings

Each serving: 200 mL (¾ cup)

1 ◆ Milk Choice (skim)	7 g carbohydrate	370 kilojoules
1 ▲ Fats & Oils Choice	6 g protein	(88 Calories)
OR	4 g fat	
1½ ◆ Milk Choices (2%)		

Variations:

Orange Creme Custard: Add 5 mL (1 tsp) grated orange rind.

Almond Creme Custard: Use 5 mL (1 tsp) almond extract in place of the vanilla extract.

Calculations as above

Citrus Banana Cheesecake

Preparation time: 15 minutes
Standing time: 2 to 4 hours

A blender is not absolutely necessary to make this creamy cheesecake if you can mash the banana and cottage cheese together until they are as smooth as possible. Pink grapefruit makes a prettier dish; however, a regular grapefruit will do.

		Crust		
250	mL	soft whole wheat breadcrumbs	1	cup
50	mL	bulk granulated brown artificial sweetener, like SugarTwin, equivalent to 50 mL (¼ cup) sugar	¼	cup
	Pinch	cardamom		Pinch
25	mL	margarine	2	tbsp
		Filling		
1		envelope unflavored gelatin	1	
175	mL	unsweetened grapefruit juice	⅔	cup
500	mL	2% cottage cheese	2	cups
1		small banana	1	
25	mL	bulk granulated artificial sweetener, like SugarTwin, equivalent to 25 mL (2 tbsp) sugar	2	tbsp
5	mL	vanilla	1	tsp
1		small pink grapefruit	1	
4		fresh strawberries, optional	4	

❶ **Crust:** In a bowl, combine bread crumbs, sweetener and cardamom. With fingers, rub in margarine. Press onto bottom of a 20 cm (8 in) springform pan.

❷ **Filling:** In a small dish or measure, sprinkle gelatin over 50 mL (¼ cup) of the grapefruit juice and let stand for 5 minutes to soften. Place dish of gelatin in pan of hot water and stir until gelatin dissolves completely. Cool to room temperature.

❸ In food processor or blender, combine cottage cheese, banana, sweetener and remaining juice. Purée until smooth. (Or, mash cottage cheese and banana with sweetener and juice or press through sieve.)

❹ Stir in dissolved gelatin and vanilla. Pour into crust.

❺ Cover and chill in refrigerator for 2 to 4 hours or until set.

❻ Remove sides from pan and with wide metal lifter, slip cheesecake off bottom of pan onto serving plate, or leave on base of springform pan.

❼ Peel grapefruit, removing all white pith. Separate segments and arrange on top of cheesecake. Slice strawberries and add to garnish if desired.

Makes 8 servings

Each serving: ⅛ of cheesecake

1	☑ Protein Choice	14 g carbohydrate	540 kilojoules
1½	◪ Fruits & Vegetables Choices	9 g protein	(128 Calories)
	OR	4 g fat	
1	☑ Protein Choice		
1	☐ Starchy Choice		

Lemon Layered Pudding

Preparation time: 10 minutes
Cooking time: 30 minutes

The surprising thing about this lemony, custard-like mixture is that it layers as it bakes. Its tart sweetness pleases both the young at heart and the young in years.

1	egg, separated	1
10 mL	granulated sugar	2 tsp
10 mL	all-purpose flour	2 tsp
	Artificial sweetener, like SugarTwin, equivalent to 30 mL (6 tsp) sugar	
10 mL	lemon juice	2 tsp
5 mL	grated lemon rind	1 tsp
125 mL	skim milk	½ cup
Pinch	cream of tartar	Pinch

❶ In a small bowl, whisk egg yolk, sugar, flour, sweetener and lemon juice. Stir in lemon rind and milk.
❷ In separate bowl, beat egg white and cream of tartar until stiff peaks form. Fold into egg yolk mixture.
❸ Pour into 2 small (200 mL/¾ cup) custard cups.
❹ Set custard cups in pan; pour in hot water to reach 2.5 cm (1 in) up sides of cups. Bake in a 160°C (325°F) oven for 30 minutes. Serve warm or cold.

Makes 2 servings

Each serving: 1 pudding, 200 mL (¾ cup)

1½	◆ Milk Choices (2%)	9 g carbohydrate	350 kilojoules
	OR	5 g protein	(83 Calories)
1	☑ Protein Choice	3 g fat	
1	◪ Fruits & Vegetables Choice		

Pumpkin Flan

Preparation time: 20 minutes
Baking time: 30 to 35 minutes
Cooling time: 10 minutes

What is pumpkin flan? It is pumpkin pie without the crust. And it is good! I serve it at Thanksgiving instead of the traditional pie. Add a dollop of whipped topping for a touch of pizzazz — however, remember to count it as an extra fat.

1	can (398 mL/14 oz) pumpkin (not pumpkin pie filling)	1
125 mL	skim milk	½ cup
175 mL	bulk granulated brown artificial sweetener, like SugarTwin, equivalent to 175 mL (⅔ cup) sugar	⅔ cup
5 mL	ground cinnamon	1 tsp
2 mL	ground ginger	½ tsp
1 mL	ground cloves	¼ tsp
1 mL	ground nutmeg	¼ tsp
50 mL	chopped pecans or walnuts	¼ cup
2	eggs	2
1	egg white	1
8	pecan halves	8

❶ Line bottom of a 20 cm (8 in) baking dish with a circle of waxed paper or parchment to fit.
❷ Combine pumpkin, milk, sweetener, cinnamon, ginger, cloves and nutmeg.
❸ Measure 125 mL (½ cup) of mixture; add chopped nuts and mix. Spread pumpkin-nut mixture over the bottom of parchment-lined baking dish.
❹ Beat eggs and egg white. Stir into remaining plain pumpkin mixture until well combined.
❺ Spoon over pumpkin-nut layer.
❻ Bake in a 180°C (350°F) oven for 30 to 35 minutes or until set (tester inserted halfway between centre and outside edge of baking dish comes out clean).
❼ Allow to cool for 10 minutes.
❽ Cut around edges with a sharp thin knife. Invert onto serving plate.
❾ Refrigerate for 1 to 2 hours to chill thoroughly.
❿ Serve garnished with pecan halves.

Makes 6 servings

Each serving: ⅙ of flan
½ 🔷 Protein Choice
1 🔶 Fruits & Vegetables Choice
1 🔺 Fats & Oils Choice

10 g carbohydrate   520 kilojoules
5 g protein   (123 Calories)
7 g fat

Apricot Sherbet

Preparation time: 5 minutes
Freezing time: 8 hours

This fruity, icy sherbet is light and lively. It helps to "cleanse the palate".

1	can (398 mL/14 oz) calorie-reduced apricots (no sugar added)	1
10 mL	bulk granulated artificial sweetener, like SugarTwin, equivalent to 10 mL (2 tsp) sugar	2 tsp

❶ Place unopened can of fruit in freezer of refrigerator for about 8 hours or overnight.
❷ Take can from freezer; open it. With a knife, cut into frozen fruit to help loosen it; then spoon frozen fruit with juice into container of food processor fitted with a steel blade; add sweetener.
❸ Process with an on/off action about 2 minutes or until puréed and slushy.
❹ Spoon immediately into chilled dessert dishes to serve immediately or transfer to a chilled plastic container, cover and store in freezer.

Makes 500 mL (2 cups) sherbet, 6 servings

Each serving: 75 mL (⅓ cup)
1 🔶 Fruits & Vegetables Choice

11 g carbohydrate   200 kilojoules
1 g protein   (48 Calories)

Variation:

Frozen Apricot Yogurt: Add 125 mL (½ cup) yogurt to the fruit and sweetener. Process until puréed. Serve immediately or transfer to plastic container, cover and freeze.

Makes 625 mL (2½ cups), 6 servings

Each serving: 100 mL (⅓ cup plus 2 tbsp)
1 🔶 Fruits & Vegetables Choice
½ 🔷 Milk Choice (2%)

13 g carbohydrate   290 kilojoules
2 g protein   (69 Calories)
1 g fat

Banana Cream Pie

Preparation time: 20 minutes
Baking time: 10 minutes

This crumb crust uses a minimum of margarine and is best if it is baked before it is filled.

	Crust		
200 mL	graham wafer crumbs	¾	cup
30 mL	margarine or butter	2	tbsp
10 mL	water	2	tsp
	Filling		
500 mL	2% or skim milk	2	cups
75 mL	cornstarch	⅓	cup
2	egg yolks OR 1 whole egg	2	
75 mL	bulk granulated artificial sweetener, like SugarTwin, equivalent to 75 mL (⅓ cup) sugar	⅓	cup
10 mL	vanilla	2	tsp
2	small bananas	2	
	Whipped topping, optional		

❶ **Crust:** In a bowl, combine crumbs, margarine and water until crumbly.
❷ With fingers, press onto the bottom and sides of a 23 cm (9 in) pie pan.
❸ Bake in a 190°C (375°F) oven for 10 minutes.
❹ **Filling:** Meanwhile, in a heavy saucepan, combine 125 mL (½ cup) of the milk and cornstarch; mix well. Add remaining milk. Place over medium heat and cook, stirring, until mixture comes to a boil; reduce heat and simmer, stirring, for 2 minutes. Remove from heat.
❺ In a bowl, beat egg yolks with a fork; add a small amount (125 mL/½ cup) of the hot mixture to beaten egg, stirring until smooth. Return immediately to hot mixture, stirring constantly. (The hot mixture will cook the egg.)
❻ Stir in sweetener and vanilla.
❼ Slice 1 banana and arrange slices on the bottom of cooled pie crust.
❽ Spoon half the pudding mixture over bananas. Slice remaining banana and arrange slices over pudding, then pour remaining pudding over bananas. Refrigerate to chill.
❾ Garnish with whipped topping, if desired, and serve.

Makes one 23 cm (9 in) pie, 6 servings

Each serving: ⅙ of pie
1 ☐ Starchy Choice
1 ◪ Fruits & Vegetables Choice
1 ▲ Fats & Oils Choice

26 g carbohydrate   770 kilojoules
4 g protein   (183 Calories)
7 g fat

Just Banana Ice Cream

Preparation time: 5 minutes
Freezing time: two 4-hour sessions

It is amazing how similar this creamy-smooth, ice-cold concoction is to soft ice cream. It is light and refreshing but it is difficult to create the fluffy light texture without the aid of a food processor.

2	small bananas	2
Pinch	ascorbic acid color keeper	Pinch
50 mL	instant skim milk powder	¼ cup
5 mL	vanilla	1 tsp
Pinch	ground cinnamon	Pinch

❶ Peel bananas; cut into thick slices and sprinkle with a pinch of ascorbic acid color keeper, wrap in plastic wrap and place in the freezer at least 4 hours or overnight until frozen solid.
❷ Unwrap bananas and place in the container of food processor fitted with metal blade. Add skim milk powder, vanilla and cinnamon. Process with an on/off motion, scraping down bowl occasionally, for about 2 minutes or until very smooth and creamy.
❸ Serve immediately or spoon into container, cover and store in freezer.

Makes 4 servings

Each serving: about 200 mL (¾ cup)
1 ◪ Fruits & Vegetables Choice
½ ◆ Milk Choice (skim)

14 g carbohydrate   270 kilojoules
2 g protein   (64 Calories)

Variation:

Strawberry Banana Ice: Add 8 fresh or unsweetened frozen strawberries to banana mixture in processor.

Calculations as above

Recipe	Food Choices Per Serving	Energy Per Serving kilojoules Calories	
Coconut Rice Pudding	1▢ Starchy; 1◆ Milk (skim)	470	113	p. 186
Apple Raisin Rice Pudding	1▢ Starchy; 1◆ Milk (skim)	400	96	p. 187
Vanilla Pudding	½▢ Starchy; 1½◆ Milk (2%)	520	123	p. 188
Chocolate Pudding	½▢ Starchy; 1½◆ Milk (2%)	520	123	p. 188
Lemon Pudding	1▢ Starchy	260	61	p. 189
Spiced Apple Pudding	1▢ Starchy; 1◣ Fruits & Vegetables	490	117	p. 190
Spiced Pineapple Pudding	1▢ Starchy; 1◣ Fruits & Vegetables	490	117	p. 190
Snow Gelatin	1✚✚ Extra	70	16	p. 191
Grape Chiffon	1◣ Fruits & Vegetables	220	52	p. 192
Strawberry Rhubarb Pie	1▢ Starchy; 1◣ Fruits & Vegetables; 1▲ Fats & Oils	750	179	p. 193
Chocolate Layered Pudding	1½◆ Milk (2%) OR 1◪ Protein; 1◣ Fruits & Vegetables	400	95	p. 194
Chocolate Mousse	1◆ Milk (homo) OR 1◆ Milk (skim); 1▲ Fats & Oils	300	72	p. 195
Chocolate Mousse Soufflé	1◆ Milk (homo); OR 1◆ Milk (skim) ½▲ Fats & Oils	320	75	p. 196
Chocolate Fondue	2◣ Fruits & Vegetables; 1▲ Fats & Oils	520	124	p. 198
Apple Clafouti	½◪ Protein; 1◣ Fruits & Vegetables	310	74	p. 199
Peach or Pear Clafouti	½◪ Protein; 1◣ Fruits & Vegetables	310	74	p. 199
Apple Butter	1◣ Fruits & Vegetables OR 1✚✚ Extra	200 / 50	48 / 12	p. 200
Vanilla Creme Custard	1½◆ Milk (2%) OR 1◆ Milk (skim) 1▲ Fats & Oils	370	88	p. 201

Recipe	Food Choices Per Serving	Energy Per Serving kilojoules Calories	
Orange Creme Custard	1½ ◆ Milk (2%) OR 1 ◆ Milk (skim); 1 ▲ Fats & Oils	370	88	p. 201
Almond Creme Custard	1½ ◆ Milk (2%) OR 1 ◆ Milk (skim) 1 ▲ Fats & Oils	370	88	p. 201
Citrus Banana Cheesecake	1 ● Protein; 1½ ◗ Fruits & Vegetables OR 1 ● Protein; 1 ☐ Starchy	540	128	p. 202
Lemon Layered Pudding	1½ ◆ Milk (2%) OR 1 ● Protein; 1 ◗ Fruits & Vegetables	350	83	p. 203
Pumpkin Flan	½ ● Protein; 1 ◗ Fruits & Vegetables 1 ▲ Fats & Oils	520	123	p. 204
Apricot Sherbet	1 ◗ Fruits & Vegetables	200	48	p. 205
Frozen Apricot Yogurt	1 ◗ Fruits & Vegetables ½ ◆ Milk (2%)	290	69	p. 205
Banana Cream Pie	1 ☐ Starchy; 1 ◗ Fruits & Vegetables 1 ▲ Fats & Oils	770	183	p. 206
Just Banana Ice Cream	½ ◆ Milk (skim); 1 ◗ Fruits & Vegetables	270	64	p. 207
Strawberry Banana Ice	½ ◆ Milk (skim); 1 ◗ Fruits & Vegetables	270	64	p. 207

Foods on the Go

All of us at times are so busy we end up eating on the run or grabbing a bite from a restaurant or fast food outlet. For a person with diabetes, that food on the run has to be right even if it is rushed.

Having each meal or snack properly balanced helps to regulate blood sugar levels during the day and keeps your energy level up. It means choosing one or more foods from each of the food groups (see chart) to make a meal with the right combination of carbohydrate, protein and fat. By choosing a variety each day, you will have a diet that contains vitamins and minerals essential for good health as well as enough food energy (Calories/kilojoules) to supply the energy you need every day to keep you healthy and active.

Eating on the go also means cafeteria food. Wherever the food is found, there are a few rules for people with diabetes and, indeed, for all people concerned with good health, to follow:

- Talk to the person taking the order and ask for your food with little or no fat — baked, broiled, poached or roasted — and salads with oily dressings "on the side" so you can control the amount you add. Most people will be helpful when they know your diet is controlled because of diabetes.
- Make up small cards with lists of food choices to keep in your pocket or pocket book. Use your list as a guide for selecting foods when you are eating away from home.
- A small carry-along form of the Good Health Eating Guide is available from the Canadian Diabetes Association and it has a place for you to write in your meal plan.
- Eat only the amount of food your food plan allows. There is no need to clean off the plate. Restaurant servings are often much too large. Share the extra, take it home in a doggy bag for another meal, or leave it on your plate.
- Just admire the gorgeous, gooey goodies. Imagine they are plastic and not good to eat.

Here are a few tips to help you make the right choice in restaurants and cafeterias:

- Nibble on a few celery sticks and radishes from the relish tray. They are considered ++ Extra Vegetables.
- Clear fat-free broths are also fine for an ++ Extra appetizer.

- Have tomato juice as a starter or a small fresh fruit cup. Remember to count either one as a ◢ Fruits & Vegetables Choice.
- Count bread, rolls, melba toast and crackers as ▢ Starchy Choices. Limit the amount you eat and don't forget the butter. It counts. It's a source of food energy that's easily forgotten, but may show up later as unwanted weight gain. Too much may interfere with the action of your insulin.
- Rely on plain greens with lemon juice as dressing for another ➕➕ Extra Vegetable.
- The best fillings for sandwiches are lean meats, poultry and slices of cheese. You can never be sure how much mayonnaise or other rich ingredients might be in filling mixtures.
- Ask for mayonnaise or relishes on the side so you can control the amount you use.
- Avoid gravies, cream cheese fillings, cream sauces, fried foods and sweet desserts at all times. Pies, pastries and puddings are full of sugar and fat.
- Fresh fruit is the best choice for dessert. Plain ice cream can be substituted for fruit and fat in your food plan on a special occasion.

Foods To Go

For a person with diabetes, it may be much easier to carry a lunch than to puzzle over what to buy from a restaurant or cafeteria. At home the pieces go together more easily because you know what your choices are. And it does not mean having peanut butter sandwiches every day.

Choose a combination of foods to equal your allowed number of food choices for a properly balanced meal, then look at the foods you can prepare from these recipes. Select ones that are easy to carry.

Some of the foods from this book are easy to take along to school or the office.

Lemonade or Limeade
Frothy Rich Hot Chocolate
Creamy Vegetable Soup
Clamato Chowder
Broccoli Soup
Paste E Fagioli
(Pasta and Beans)
Keeps-A-Week Coleslaw

Chick Pea and Tomato Salad
Tuna Turnovers
Meatball Ragout
Lime-Broiled or Poached
   Chicken
Mexican Beans and Rice
Lentil Curry

If the carting back and forth can be handled, a wide-mouthed Thermos container is perfect for hot or cold dishes. A small 250 mL (1 cup) one for drinks will solve the beverage problem.

It is also smart to include any mid-morning or mid-afternoon snacks, from your food plan, in your packed lunch. Or non-perishable snacks for a whole week can be packed at the beginning of the week and kept at school.

If you are at school, let your teacher or coach know about your need for a snack. If you prefer not to eat your snack in the classroom or on the playing field, you can be excused for the short time necessary to eat.

Brown Bag Totable Lunches that Work

1. Hard-cooked egg, salad in Thermos, muffin and fruit
2. Hearty soup in a Thermos, scones, fruit, Butterscotch Peanut Cookies
3. Cottage cheese with crunchy greens like celery and green pepper, small whole wheat roll, milk and fruit
4. Pita sandwiches filled with sliced meat, poultry or cheese; raw cauliflower and broccoli florets, milk and fresh fruit in a Thermos
5. Leftover dinner in a Thermos, zucchini sticks, Apricot Loaf and yogurt
6. Eggnog, muffin and fruit
7. Fresh fruit, muffin, cheese, celery sticks, milk

Index